Acts

DAILY BIBLE COMMENTARY

A Guide for Reflection and Prayer

Acts

Loveday Alexander

HENDRICKSON
PUBLISHERS

Acts
Daily Bible Commentary
Hendrickson Publishers, Inc.
P. O. Box 3473
Peabody, Massachusetts 01961-3473

ISBN 978-1-59856-189-0

Printed in the United States of America

First Printing — April 2007

Library of Congress Cataloging-in-Publication Data

Alexander, Loveday.
        Acts / Loveday Alexander.
            p. cm. — (The Daily Bible commentary ; 5)
        ISBN 978-1-59856-189-0 (alk. paper)
        1. Bible. N.T. Acts—Commentaries. 2. Bible. N.T. Acts—
    Devotional literature. I. Title.
        BS2625.53.A44 2007
        226.6′077—dc22
                                                    2007004003

Introducing the
Daily Bible Commentary
Series
A Guide for Reflection and Prayer

Congratulations! You are embarking on a voyage of discovery—or re-discovery. You may feel you know the Bible very well; you may never have turned its pages before. You may be looking for a fresh way of approaching daily Bible study; you may be searching for useful insights to share in a study group or from a pulpit.

The Daily Bible Commentary series is designed for all those who want to study the Scriptures in a way that will warm the heart as well as instruct the mind.

- If you have never really studied the Bible before, the series offers a serious yet accessible way in.

- If you want to have both head and heart knowledge of the Bible, the series helps you first understand what the Bible is saying and then reflect on its meaning in your life and in the way you pray.

- If you help to lead a church study group, or are otherwise involved in regular preaching and teaching, you can find invaluable "snapshots" of a Bible passage through the Daily Bible Commentary approach.

- If you are a church worker or pastor, looking to recharge your faith, this series could help you recover the wonder of Scripture.

To help you, the series distills the best of scholarly insights into straightforward language and devotional emphasis. Explanation of background material and discussion of the original Greek and Hebrew will always aim to be brief.

Using a Daily Bible Commentary

The series is designed for use alongside any version of the Bible. You may have your own favorite translation, but you might like to consider trying a different one in order to gain fresh perspectives on familiar passages.

Many Bible translations come in a range of editions, including study and reference editions that have concordances, various kinds of special indexes, maps, and marginal notes. These can all prove helpful in studying the relevant passage.

The Daily Bible Commentaries are designed to be used on a daily basis, with you reading a short passage from the Bible and then learning more about it from the commentary entry. Alternatively, it can be read straight through, or it can be used as a resource book for insight into particular verses of the biblical book.

While it is important to deepen our understanding of a given passage, this series always aims to engage both heart and mind in the study of the Bible. The Scriptures point to our Lord himself and our task is to use them to build our relationship with him. When we read, let us do so prayerfully, slowly, reverently, expecting God to speak to our very being.

Contents

ACKNOWLEDGMENTS

My thanks are due to Richard Burridge, Naomi Starkey and the editorial board of *The People's Bible Commentary* for their support, encouragement (and patience!) with this project over the past few years, and to all my colleagues and students in the world of Acts scholarship with whom it has been a pleasure to engage in this fascinating study. But this volume is really addressed to all my friends outside the university with whom I have tried (over the year) to discover what Acts might mean for 21st-century Christians, and I would like to dedicate it to Canon Brian Young and the congregation of St Philip's, Alderley Edge (especially the ecumenical Bible study group), in whose company I have learnt more than I can say of what it means to read God's living word in today's world. Keep on studying—and keep on asking awkward questions!

ACTS: INTRODUCTION

*Bilbo often used to say that there was only one Road; that it was like a
great river: its springs were at every doorstep, and every path was its
tributary. 'It's a dangerous business, Frodo, going out of your door,' he used
to say. 'You step into the Road, and if you don't keep your feet, there is no
knowing where you might be swept off to.'*

Tolkien 1966, p. 83

Welcome to the journey!

'This book will make a traveller of thee,' says John Bunyan at the
beginning of *The Pilgrim's Progress*; and the same could well be said of
the Acts of the Apostles. Acts is the story of a journey. It tells the story
of the birth of the Church, and its journey outwards and across the
world from where it all began, in an upstairs room in Jerusalem.
Woven into this story are the journeys of a whole host of individual
travellers, apostles and others, moving back and forth across that
Mediterranean world and spreading the word wherever they go. But
it's also the story of the journey of faith, a journey to which every
reader is invited: it's no accident that one of Luke's favourite
metaphors for discipleship is 'the Way'.

   As so often in the Bible, the journey starts with a vision, which
empowers and controls the travellers and to which they constantly
revert. The story begins on a mountain-top, the classic location for
vision in the Bible, where the heavens open and angels and mortals
speak face to face (ch. 1). Then comes the communal visionary experience of Pentecost, when the empowerment of God's Spirit becomes
something visible even to the crowds in a Jerusalem street (ch. 2).
Further into the narrative, the two controlling visions are Peter's rooftop trance (ch. 10) and Paul's encounter with the risen Christ on the
Damascus road (ch. 9); each is recounted over and over again, as the
characters in the story are challenged to unravel the true significance
of what God is saying to them (chs. 11; 15; 22; 26). And vision provides not only the starting point for mission but also its content: 'we
cannot but speak of the things which we have seen and heard' (4:20;
26:19).

Journey into outer space

Like any road movie, Acts contains a strong geographical element. It's the one book in the New Testament where you really need to keep an eye on the map. Most Bibles include a map of 'The Journeys of St Paul', and there are excellent maps available in Bible atlases and other guides. (Tip: a modern physical map of the eastern Mediterranean will often give you a much better flavour of the terrain covered in the book.) More than any other book of the New Testament, Acts conveys a sense of the excitement and romance of travel. It's a cosmopolitan book, moving with ease from the narrow streets of Jerusalem to the classical elegance of Athens, from the high passes of the Turkish-Syrian border to the back streets of Rome. And on the way we meet a variety of deftly drawn characters, from the Ethiopian court treasurer (ch. 8) to the friendly Roman centurion Julius (ch. 27). Acts reminds us that there's a big wide world out there—a daunting prospect to the Galilean disciples on the Mount of Olives, as Jesus gives them their marching orders (1:8). But gradually, as we read, we come to share with them the unfolding excitement of finding that God is out there too, waiting to meet them and surprise them in this strange world that is also God's world.

Journey into inner space

There's also a more hidden journey, a journey of discovery in which the familiar turns out to be more surprising than we thought. 'Who will show me the way?' asks the Ethiopian, sitting in his chariot on the Gaza road and poring over an ancient scroll (8:31). It's not a road map he's asking for but a new way to read the age-old scriptures, and that's what Philip provides (8:35). Acts conducts its characters (and therefore its readers) into an inner journey of exploration under the guidance of God's Holy Spirit, working out how the 'this' of personal experience corresponds with the 'that' of God's revelation. This is not always an easy thing to do. Often it means facing up to the puzzlement and hostility of our closest compatriots. Even harder, it means confronting our own prejudices and facing up to our own persistent refusal to recognize God's Spirit at work. So there's a lot of conflict built into the story of Acts; and some of the shortest journeys in the book, geographically speaking, turn out to be some of the longest and most significant in terms of inner space.

A guide for time travellers

This commentary is designed as a kind of interactive travel guide for readers of Acts, helping you to relate to Luke's story on three levels.

My first priority is to describe the journey itself from the point of view of the author and his first readers, taking pains to listen carefully to the story as he tells it, to pick up the clues he has laid for informed readers, and to try first of all to understand the story in its own terms. This is a basic courtesy we owe to any book, especially to a book written 2000 years ago in a very different culture from our own. That means trying to experience the journey from the viewpoint of the characters in Luke's story, hearing the conversations and debates from inside, trying to understand both sides before jumping to conclusions about what's going on. It also means trying to hear Luke's story through the ears of his original readers, asking about the literary echoes or political resonances that would be picked up by a first-century audience.

Secondly, we can take a step back and ask how Luke's story relates to other stories we know of from that time and place. This means filling in some of the historical information we need, to understand the significance of Luke's story: who was this emperor or that official? What else was going on at the time? How does Luke's version of events tie in with other evidence—Paul's letters, for example? I have tried to indicate what the main historical questions are and where you can find out more if you want to.

And thirdly, we need to move back into the 21st century (which of course we never really left) and ask how Luke's story relates to our own stories. There are many different kinds of travel guides, but most of them fall into two categories: those that offer an armchair substitute for travel, and those that incite you to get out there and sample the real thing. My hope and prayer is that readers will find this guide provoking in many different ways, and that you will be able to use it to inform and inspire your own journeying on the Way, whether individually or as a group. So each reading ends with a question, a quotation or a prayer, suggesting ways to link up with some of the stories that belong to our lives today—things that are happening in the newspapers, or in our churches, or in our own spiritual lives. Use these any way you want, and treat them as a springboard to make your own connections between Luke's world and ours—or simply as a framework for your own prayers.

Basic orientation

The rest of this Introduction will deal with the basic information and equipment you need for the journey. You may like to read it all before starting, or you may prefer to save it up and refer back to it as the need arises.

The author

Like most New Testament scholars, I use the name 'Luke' as short-hand for 'the author of Acts—whoever that was'. This is the name that has been attached to the third Gospel and Acts from earliest times, both in the manuscript tradition and in the early church writers who quote him. But it's worth pausing at the outset to ask what we know about the person who put this crucial story together —and what kind of detective work has gone into piecing the story together.

First, we know from Acts 1:1 that the author has already written a book about Jesus—and it doesn't take much detective ability to work out that this 'former treatise' is the third Gospel, which is dedicated to the same person, Theophilus, and is written in very much the same style. So 'Luke' is actually the author of two books, which together make up almost a quarter of the whole New Testament. And our author tells us a bit more about himself in the preface to the Gospel, at Luke 1:1–4. This preface doesn't give the author's name (although the masculine participle used in verse 3 does tell us that he was male). In some ways the preface tells us more about who Luke was not than who he was: he wasn't the first to write down the story of Jesus (v. 1); he wasn't an eyewitness (v. 2). But the whole way he writes tells us quite a bit about the sort of person he was: rational, business-like, reassuringly pragmatic, full of words like 'carefully', 'accurately', 'thoroughly', 'in an orderly fashion' (vv. 3–4). It's as if Luke wants to reassure his readers that the extraordinary story they're about to read is one that belongs in the real world, a world of people like Theophilus who like to check out the reliability of what they're told (v. 4)—in other words, a world of people like you and me.

Nevertheless, this sober, rational author is not standing outside the story he tells, like an investigative journalist. He has a personal stake in it. The 'we' of the preface to Luke's Gospel aligns the writer with the whole Christian tradition, with all those who have received the testimony of the original eyewitnesses (v. 2). In fact, he's part of the community in which the whole extraordinary business has come to pass (v. 1). And towards the end of his second volume, the 'we' slips in again in a way that implies that the author is actually part of the story he narrates (Acts 16:10–17; 20:5–15; 21:1–18; 27:1—28:16). It sounds as if our author was one of those who accompanied Paul on his travels, including the last, fateful trip to Rome. If so, all we need to do is to work out from Paul's letters which of Paul's many friends and co-workers is the most likely candidate for the job. It seems safe to assume that the author isn't any of the people he mentions in the third person (Barnabas, Timothy, Gaius, and so on—you can work it out for yourself if you want to). That still leaves quite a few options: Paul had a lot of friends! (Look at Romans 16, for example.) But as far back as we can see (as early as Irenaeus, writing around AD180), the favoured candidate is the attractive if shadowy figure of the beloved physician of Paul's prison epistles, the co-worker who sends greetings to the house churches in Colossae, the faithful Luke who sticks with the apostle in prison: look up Philemon 24; Colossians 4:14; 2 Timothy 4:11.

Not all scholars accept that this detective work has come up with the right answer. Some would argue that the 'we-passages' of Acts are just a literary device, or that the author has incorporated some genuine diary entries from one of Paul's companions. Many find it hard to believe that a close companion of Paul could have written Acts, on the grounds that the Paul whom Luke portrays is actually rather different from the Paul who comes across from his letters. That's an issue we shall look at from time to time in the second half of Acts, but for my part (in common with a number of other recent commentators), I find that on balance the traditional authorship is the simplest way to account for all the data. Not that Luke's viewpoint is identical with that of Paul's letters in every respect. Luke hardly ever calls Paul an apostle, for example, and (as we shall see) he has certainly been selective in the story he tells. But then, which of our closest friends would portray any of us exactly as we would like to portray ourselves?

Ultimately, I don't believe that the name of the author is what really matters. Much more important is to work out why the author has shaped his story in the particular way he has. For that, it is highly significant that the author (let's stick with calling him Luke) has chosen to align himself with the first-hand experience of Paul's travelling companions. And that, I believe, provides a vital clue to the distinctive viewpoint that gives his story its shape.

The shape of Luke's story

It's helpful to think of Luke's story as a drama in four acts. The first three correspond roughly to the threefold geographical plan outlined in Jesus' commission in 1:8: Jerusalem (Act I: chapters 1—7); Judea and Samaria (Act II: chapters 8—12); 'to the ends of the earth' (Act III: chapters 13—19). Act IV (chapters 20—28) brings Paul back to Jerusalem, and tells how he eventually ended up travelling to Rome as a prisoner.

Looking forward, in other words, the story proceeds like a series of chain reactions (Pentecost; persecution; mission), each one triggering the next. As we watch each explosion, it's impossible to predict where the debris will end up: the potential is global (2:9–11), and Luke doesn't attempt to tell all the stories that his narrative opens up. (What happened to all the other apostles, or the other deacons?) But unrolling the story backwards, it's quite easy to see how each step links back to the one before. Starting out from the Mount of the Ascension, there's no way you could predict Paul's imprisonment in Rome, but if you begin at the end you can trace the causal links all the way back. And the wonderful thing that Luke wants to impress above all on his readers is how each step—even the apparent disasters—is under the guidance of God's Holy Spirit. Like Joseph, Paul could have said, 'It was God who brought me here to preach the life-giving gospel of salvation' (compare Genesis 45:5).

So in many respects the easiest way to understand the shape of the drama is to begin at the end. 'And *that's* how we got to Rome!' says Luke triumphantly, after all the excitement of the shipwreck (28:14) —as if the whole point of his story is to explain how Paul comes to be arriving in Rome, accompanied by a Roman centurion, charged with disrupting the peace and generally causing mayhem back in Jerusalem. In fact, I believe that is precisely Luke's point. The whole last quarter of the book tells the long and complicated story of the riot in the temple that triggered it all off, and the series of trials in which Paul has to defend himself before the Jewish and Roman authorities. But of course we want to know how he came to be in the temple in the first place, and why he got people so wound up: so that takes us back into Act III, which tells the extraordinary story of Paul's mission, and how he kept trying to give his message to Jewish audiences around the Mediterranean world and then finding that he was being pushed into giving it to the Gentiles too. But Paul wasn't acting just under his own steam: Act II takes us further back, to the heavenly revelation that stopped Paul in his tracks and made him a follower of Jesus instead of a persecutor of Jesus' disciples, and shows how Paul's story ties in with the stories of other people following this Way that people call 'the sect of the Nazarenes' (24:5, 14). And that takes us, finally, to Act I (chapters 1—7), which tells the story of how the sect originated and its links with the hidden substratum of Acts, the good news that God has sent salvation for the whole world in Jesus, the Christ (compare Luke 1:68–79; 24:44–47).

Journey's end

The final scene of Acts also provides a vital clue to Luke's original audience and situation. Luke tells us a lot about Paul the missionary, preaching to the Gentile world (in Act III), and Paul the prisoner, making his defence before the Roman empire (in Act IV). In the final scene of the book, however, Paul is neither of these. His final words are addressed to the leaders of the Jewish community in Rome, who ask him (in surprisingly neutral tones), 'Tell us about this sect.' In essence, I believe that Luke's whole story is the answer to that question— although my hunch is (along with most scholars) that Luke is actually writing after Paul's death, and after the destructive and futile rebellion against Rome that left the temple in ruins.

The final scene of Acts is a kind of freeze-frame that encapsulates a key moment in the long, fraught history of Jewish-Christian relations. Acts records three decades of dialogue, debate and division—sometimes violent—over 'the Way' within the Jewish community. Much of this dialogue takes place on the margins, in the border zones where different groups within the Jewish family are jostling for position, each at times trying to edge the others out. So there are times when Luke speaks of 'the Jews' as outsiders, and times (much more often) when Paul and Peter address their fellow Jews as insiders in impassioned, prophetic appeal. That's the time-warp Acts is caught up in, a freeze-frame that's hard to recapture from where we stand today. But I believe it is essential that we give full weight to all the voices in that dialogue, within and outside the church, refusing to foreclose the debate—which in many ways foreshadows the debates going on in the church today between innovation and continuity, 'traditional' and 'emerging' patterns of church life. In our ready identification with one side or the other, with the prodigal or the elder brother, it's all too easy to shut out the voice of the Father who says to both brothers, 'Son, you are always with me, and all that I have is yours' (Luke 15:31).

For information and further reading

Because this dialogue within the Jewish community is so important as a framework for Acts, we need to draw on a range of contemporary sources to understand what is going on in first-century Judaism, and how that fits into the wider world of the Roman empire. I have included a minimum of source references in the notes, but you may like to follow up some further reading to get the flavour of Luke's world. All the books listed here will provide a portal for further exploration of current Acts research if you are so inclined. If you're not, just ignore them!

- Probably the most accessible single resource for reading Acts in its historical context is the splendid 5-volume set on *The Book of Acts in Its First-Century Setting* edited by Bruce Winter and Andrew Clarke (Eerdmans, 1993–96). This contains up-to-date summaries of recent findings on such matters as house churches, Roman roads, magistrates and 'God-fearers', as well as essays by leading scholars on literary and theological issues in Acts.

- One of the most significant finds for enlarging our understanding of the world of first-century Judaism is the Dead Sea Scrolls. The Scrolls, and the Qumran community that read them, throw a fascinating light on some of the practices of the Jerusalem church, such as the casting of lots and the community of goods. The Scrolls are easily available in English translation (Vermes 1997). There are many good scholarly introductions: I'd recommend Campbell (2002) and Brooke (2005a, 2005b).

- Much of the argument of Acts turns on the interpretation of scripture. Luke and his contemporaries in the Greek-speaking diaspora read the Bible not in Hebrew but in Greek, following a translation made by Jewish scholars over the last few centuries before Christ. This Greek Bible is often referred to as the Septuagint (LXX for short), from the Greek word for '70'. The name derives from the legend that the translation was made by 70 scholars working independently but coming up (miraculously) with identical results. Dines (2004) provides an excellent short introduction.

- Outside the Bible, our main historical source for events in first-century Palestine is the Jewish historian Josephus, who took part in the great Jewish war against Rome in AD66–70, and wrote up his memoirs in Rome at the end of the first century. Josephus' great history of the Jewish War is available in English in the *Penguin Classics* series, as are Roman writers like Tacitus, Suetonius and Pliny.

- Commentaries on Acts are numerous. The 'big four' reference commentaries of the last decade are Barrett (1994, 1998), Fitzmyer (1998), Johnson (1992) and Witherington (1998). Of the shorter, more accessible commentaries, I'd recommend especially Gaventa (2003). The Word commentary (Walton) and my own Black's commentary are due to appear within the next few years, and a collection of my own essays on the literary world of Acts appears in Alexander (2005).

- Finally, there have been some exciting publications in the last few years dealing with the theological issues raised by studying Acts within the life of today's worldwide Church. I have benefited enormously from the work of Gonzalez (2001) and Johnson (1996), and from an advance look at Robinson and Wall (2006). Gallagher and Hertig (2004) also suggest some imaginative connections between the world of Acts and the worldwide Church today, as does the introduction to Alison (2003).

Source references

Alexander 2005: Loveday C.A. Alexander, *Acts in Its Ancient Literary Context: A Classicist Looks at the Acts of the Apostles* (T&T Clark International.

Alison 2003: James Alison, *On Being Liked* (Crossroad).

Barrett 1994, 1998: C.K. Barrett, *The Acts of the Apostles* (2 volumes, International Critical Commentary, T&T Clark).

Brooke 2005a: George Brooke, *Qumran and the Jewish Jesus* (Grove Books).

Brooke 2005b: George Brooke, *The Dead Sea Scrolls and the New Testament* (Fortress).

Buchan n.d: John Buchan, *The Four Adventures of Richard Hannay* (Hodder & Stoughton).

Campbell 2002: Jonathan G. Campbell, *Deciphering the Dead Sea Scrolls* (2nd ed., Blackwell).

Casson 1999: Lionel Casson, *Travel in the Ancient World* (Johns Hopkins University Press).

Fitzmyer 1998: Joseph A. Fitzmyer SJ, *The Acts of the Apostles* (Anchor Bible, Doubleday).

Dines 2005: Jennifer M. Dines, *The Septuagint* (T&T Clark International, Continuum).

Gallagher and Hertig 2004: Robert Gallagher and Paul Hertig (eds.), *Mission in Acts: Ancient Narratives in Contemporary Context* (Orbis).

Gaventa 2003: Beverly R. Gaventa, *Acts* (Abingdon NT Commentary, Abingdon).

Gonzalez 2001: Justo Gonzalez, *Acts: The Gospel of the Spirit* (Orbis).

Green 1995: Joel B. Green, *The Theology of the Gospel of Luke* (Cambridge University Press).

Jackson and Wright 1999: Peter Jackson & Chris Wright, *Faith Confirmed* (SPCK).

Johnson 1992: Luke Timothy Johnson, *The Acts of the Apostles* (Sacra Pagina, Liturgical Press).

Johnson 1996: Luke Timothy Johnson, *Scripture and Discernment: Decision Making in the Church* (rev. ed., Abingdon Press).

Nouwen 1989: Henri Nouwen, *Seeds of Hope* (Darton, Longman & Todd).

Pirsig 2000: Robert M. Pirsig, *Zen and the Art of Motorcycle Maintenance* (Perennial Classics).

Ranken 1998: Michael D. Ranken, 'A theology for the priest at work', in James M.M. Francis and Leslie D. Francis (eds.), *Tentmaking: Perspectives on Self-Supporting Ministry* (Gracewing).

Robinson & Wall 2006: Anthony B. Robinson and Robert W. Wall, *Called to be Church: The Book of Acts for a New Day* (Eerdmans).

Tolkien 1966: J.R.R. Tolkien, *The Lord of the Rings: The Fellowship of the Ring* (Allen & Unwin).

Vermes 1997: Geza Vermes, *The Complete Dead Sea Scrolls in English* (Allen Lane/Penguin).

Wild Goose 1999: Wild Goose Worship Group, *A Wee Worship Book* (Wild Goose Resource Group).

Winter & Clarke 1993–96: Bruce Winter and Andrew Clarke (eds.), *The Book of Acts in Its First-century Setting* (5 volumes, Paternoster/ Eerdmans).

Witherington 1998: Ben Witherington III, *The Acts of the Apostles: A Socio-Rhetorical Commentary* (Eerdmans).

1

ACT ONE: JERUSALEM

When the Lord restored the fortunes of Zion, we were like those who dream.
Then our mouth was filled with laughter, and our tongue with shouts of joy;
then they said among the nations, 'The Lord has done great things for them.'
The Lord has done great things for us; we are glad. (Psalm 126:1–3, RSV)

The opening chapters of Acts capture something of the dream-like
quality of the psalmist's vision of the restoration of Zion. Restoration,
and the fulfilment of the age-old promises, is very much what the first
quarter of the book is about. But restoration is also about repentance,
and that is what is on offer for the people of Jerusalem and their rulers.

The story so far

Like the preface to Luke's Gospel (Luke 1:1–4), the opening verse of
Acts is essentially a kind of label stuck on to the front of the book, in
which the author momentarily speaks in his own voice and addresses
the reader direct. The practical reason for putting the label here is that
each of Luke's two volumes is about the right length for a scroll, so this
point marks the break. Because a scroll has no spine or dust jacket,
ancient authors normally used the first sentence to supply the essential information that readers needed to identify what they were reading.
The effect is rather like changing reels halfway through the film in an
old-fashioned cinema. For a few moments we slip out of the narrative
world and back into the real world of authors and readers.

Volume Two

The first thing we learn as we open the book is that it's the second
volume of a diptych, the second half of a book that describes 'all that
Jesus did and taught from the beginning' (v. 1). And it's not just a
loosely connected sequel. It's easy to see from the first verse that Luke
expects his readers to know what has happened in the Gospel. He
makes very few concessions to new readers: there are no footnotes or
helpful glosses to tell them who John or the apostles were. Everything
in the second volume, Acts, presupposes the story of the first (that is,
the story of Jesus) and there are all sorts of links and connections that
observant readers can pick up between the two.

22

Captain and crew

The preface also lays the groundwork in important ways for the second half of Luke's story. It introduces the key characters of Acts, beginning with Jesus himself. Luke's story of Jesus is shaped in a particular way, focused on the actions and teachings of a holy man (v. 1), just as many Greek biographies described the actions and teachings of a philosopher. That story is directed towards the ascension (v. 2), which creates the centrepoint for the whole two-volume work. For Luke, the ascension of Jesus is not an afterthought, tacked on to tidy up the end of the narrative: the passion, resurrection and ascension are a unit, beginning as far back as Luke 9:51. But the story doesn't end with Jesus' departure to heaven: the opening scene of Acts creates a double overlay with the last chapter of the Gospel (Luke 24), both describing in different ways the captain's final instructions to his crew. In a sense, everything in Acts stems from this moment. In the chapters that ensue, we shall follow the apostles' attempts to carry out the mission Jesus has entrusted to them.

The apostles and the Spirit

The apostles (v. 2) are therefore the next most important characters. We shall hear much more about them as the story progresses, but this brief introduction already tells us that they were chosen by Jesus and instructed by Jesus—companions who shared table-fellowship with him (the meaning of 'staying with them' in v. 4, NRSV). The essence of their commission lies precisely in being entrusted with the unique experience of seeing Jesus alive after his passion (v. 3), witnessing the 'many convincing proofs' of his resurrection life. Transmitting this experience to an unbelieving world, offering living proof of Jesus' continued (but hidden) resurrection life, is what they are about. They are not alone: Jesus' instruction is 'in the Holy Spirit' who has been with him since the beginning of the Gospel story (Luke 1:35; 3:22; 4:14). And more is on its way: the promise of the Father (compare Luke 24:49) is about to be realized not many days from now (vv. 4–5). There's a sense of expectancy here which takes us right back to the beginning of the Gospel.

PRAYER

Lord Jesus, as we read the story of the apostles, help us to catch a glimpse of what it means to be your disciples, and to take our place in your mission in the world.

2

On the HOLY MOUNTAIN

Most prefaces of this type move rather prosaically from 'What I've just told you' to 'What I'm going to tell you' in a matching sentence. Luke gives his readers a much more dramatic and vivid preview of the book we're about to read. Already in 1:4 he has drawn us in unexpectedly to eavesdrop on Jesus' conversations with his disciples in those last 40 days. Now we find ourselves standing beside them, in the mountain-top vision that powers the whole of the narrative of Acts.

Restoring the kingdom

First, Jesus has to redirect the apostles (and, with them, ourselves) from looking back to looking forward, and to a rather different kind of future from the one they (and perhaps we) expect. The air of expectancy that pervades this opening scene rekindles the eschatological expectations of the coming kingdom in Luke 3—but God's future is very different. The disciples ask, 'Is this the time to restore the kingdom to Israel?' (v. 6). 'Yes,' is the answer: God is about to act, and Israel is being offered restoration—but with a difference. Its timing is not something we need to worry about (v. 7). The Christian is to live in a constant state of alertness and expectancy, without knowing exactly when the end will be. What we do have is empowerment for the present task (v. 8)—'you will receive power when the Holy Spirit has come upon you'—and with the promise comes a glimpse of the immense and daunting task ahead. This is the first hint that travel is going to be important in the apostles' story: verse 8 gives a threefold geographical shape to the story of Acts, which we shall see gradually unfolding in the mission to Jerusalem (chs. 1—7), to Judea and Samaria (chs. 8—12), and 'to the ends of the earth' (chs. 13—28).

On the mountain-top

It is only in verse 12 that we learn that the ascension takes place on a mountain. As mountains go, the Mount of Olives is a relatively insignificant height overlooking the city of Jerusalem, but it is the only mountain mentioned in Acts (apart from Stephen's reference to

Mount Sinai in 7:30), and, like Mount Sinai, it is a place of immense theological significance. Traditional icons of the transfiguration show Jesus at the top of a very sharp and pointy mountain, with the disciples prostrated in attitudes of awe and wonder at his feet—a classic attempt to fix in paint the intersection of the eternal with time, a moment with no before and after. But (as in a cartoon) some versions of the icon also show Jesus and the disciples precisely in those 'before' and 'after' moments, with Jesus leading the disciples up the mountain on the left-hand side, and shooing them down again on the right. That, to me, is how Luke's picture of the ascension works. Right at the heart of his two-volume narrative is a mountain-top scene, where Jesus is seen in his glory and taken up into heaven. It's a moment of vision (note the four different words for 'seeing' in verses 9–11), where the disciples (eleven of them this time) are finally vouchsafed a glimpse of the true nature and destination of this person whose company they have been sharing over the last three years—before the cloud tantalizingly hides him from their sight (v. 9).

Down the mountain

Acts is also the narrative of a journey. Ever since Luke 9:51, Jesus has been leading his disciples along the way that leads to his 'taking up', teaching them, bearing with their failings and leading them to an end that seems progressively darker—until the single moment of revelation comprised in the double action of resurrection and ascension. Now the way leads down the mountain again, downwards and outwards from the defining moment of revelation, back into the mundane world of argument and doubt. It's not an easy transition to make: it's much easier to stand 'gazing up towards heaven' (v. 10). On the mount of transfiguration, Peter had insanely proposed setting up a campsite (Luke 9:33), until the cloud faded and they found themselves alone on the misty mountain-side, with only Jesus there to show them the way back down to earth. This time, they won't have that consoling human presence: they will have to discover new ways of experiencing his presence. At the moment, all they can feel is absence. Yet, there's a task to perform—and a promise to hold on to (v. 11).

PRAYER

Lord Jesus, help us to follow wherever you lead, and to know your presence every step of the way.

3

ACTS 1:13-26

The MISSING APOSTLE

This whole scene has an air of the interim about it, an air of focused expectancy, waiting obediently for... what? There is some unfinished business to be resolved before the narrative proper gets under way: the problem of the apostle who wasn't.

Retracing steps

When you have no guidance over where to go next, the sensible thing is to stay put (compare Luke 24:49). For the disciples who had come up from Galilee those few short weeks before, the upstairs room (v. 13) must have seemed like a sanctuary in a suddenly hostile and empty city, a room full of memories of a vivid and urgent presence, now bafflingly withdrawn. Luke gives us here a strategic reminder of the names of the original disciples from Galilee (compare Luke 6:14–16), minus one. But the eleven disciples are not the only members of this fledgling community. In fact, we learn from verse 15 that there are up to 120 people in that first fellowship, all persevering in prayer (v. 14). When there's no way forward, that's always a good idea!

Sisters and brothers

Luke singles out two other groups here (v. 14). The 'women' could refer to the wives of the disciples, but more probably means the band of women supporters who had followed Jesus from Galilee (Luke 8:1–3) and who, in all the Gospels, play an important role in the resurrection narratives (Luke 23:55—24:11). This particular group has no role in Luke's ongoing story (he makes it clear that only men can act as witnesses to the resurrection), but women, named and unnamed, will continue to play a significant part in the development of the early church (5:1–11; 6:1; 8:3; 9:36–42; 12:12–16; 16:11–15; 18:1–4, 26; 21:5).

Then there are Mary the mother of Jesus, and his brothers. This is the first and last mention of Mary in Acts. The brothers of Jesus also are not mentioned again as a group, although James will play a significant role later on (see comment on 15:12–21; 21:18–30).

Luke goes out of his way to stress the togetherness of the three groups (the Eleven, the women and Jesus' family) at the outset, and the fact that they acted in concert in the choice of a replacement apostle.

The twelfth apostle

The list of names in verse 13 ends with a yawning gap—Judas, named as the betrayer in Luke 6:16 (compare Luke 22:21). Judas is both an embarrassment and a theological conundrum. Peter, taking his first steps into a leadership role here (v. 15), doesn't balk the issue. Judas was 'numbered among us', and 'was allotted his share in this ministry' (v. 17): in other words, he *was* an apostle, sent and commissioned just like the others. Luke is quite realistic about the possibility of failure within the holy community (see the story of Ananias in ch. 5). In fact, he adds a footnote at this point (vv. 18–19 is clearly Luke speaking, not Peter), which highlights Judas' fate as an awful warning to the later community. Nevertheless (and this is the first appearance of a recurrent theme in Acts), Judas' failure was 'foretold by scripture'; in other words, it was part of God's purpose (vv. 16, 20). The scriptural verses that Peter cites to make his point (v. 20, citing Psalms 69:25; 109:8) are essentially descriptions of a life alienated from God; but Peter uses them to highlight the fact that the 'office' Judas held, the ministry he shared in, is more important than the individual and can survive his failure.

There is, then, a vacancy, and it is the job of this assembly to fill it. The qualifications are clearly described (vv. 21–22): being with Jesus from the beginning, plus the willingness to 'become a witness'. In other words, witness-ship does not depend simply on what you've seen but also on your willingness to speak out about it. This last point may explain why women are disqualified from the position: women were not legally accepted as witnesses in Jewish law.

There is no shortage of qualified candidates (v. 23), so a mechanism has to be found for making a choice. Casting lots (v. 26) is a nice combination of human action (something must be done) and divine will. The casting of lots never appears again in Acts as a mechanism for selection, but it was a recognized means of discovering the divine will both in ancient Judaism (especially at Qumran) and in the Greek civic process. This is not a resort to mere chance, however: the essence of the process is prayer (vv. 24–25).

PRAYER

Father, teach us to persevere in prayer when we can't see the way forward.

4

The Spirit Comes

The denouement, when it comes, is as dramatic as it is unexpected. After the preliminaries, the sense of expectancy in chapter 1, this scene makes the beginning of the drama proper, the first 'big' scene of Acts. It follows a threefold pattern that we shall see more than once: a theophany, a dramatic revelatory event in which God acts directly to make himself known; followed by diverse reactions, for and against; followed by explanation in which the characters go back to the Hebrew scriptures to make sense of what is happening.

The day of Pentecost

First comes the event itself, described with dramatic ceremony and in richly scriptural language. Pentecost (v. 1) comes 50 days after Passover, so this date fixes the outpouring of the Spirit precisely to ten days after the ascension (1:3) and seven weeks after the crucifixion (Luke 22:1), details which would eventually determine the shape of the Christian liturgical year. Pentecost was originally a harvest festival, the feast of Weeks (Hebrew: *Shavuot*), thanking God for the first grain of the new harvest (see Deuteronomy 16:9–10; Leviticus 23:15–16). By Luke's time, however, it had also come to be associated with the giving of the law on Mount Sinai, and with the renewing of the covenant at Qumran. The Temple Scroll from Qumran speaks of three successive 'Pentecost' feasts of new grain, new wine, and new oil. So, for Luke and his first readers, this is a day rich with symbolic resonances. It is the day when God chooses to 'fulfil' everything that this multi-layered festival points to: thanksgiving and celebration for the outpouring of God's blessings on the life of his people, and the renewal of God's covenant with his people and of their commitment to living as God's people in the world.

Wind and fire

What happens exactly? Luke uses several words to stress the togetherness of Jesus' followers on this occasion (v. 1), which makes it look as if he means to include all the 120 believers of 1:14–15 (including Jesus' family and the women), not just the Twelve. What they heard must have been frightening to an indoor gathering, busy trying to keep themselves quiet. It sounds like the noise of a powerful, dynamic blast of wind (not a gentle breeze!), filling the house (v. 2), a blast that brings to mind the biblical evocations of God's wind buffeting the mountaintops (1 Kings 19:11; compare Psalm 29:9), or God's breath blowing life into dead bodies (Genesis 2:7; Ezekiel 37): the words for 'spirit' in Hebrew and Greek (*ruach*, *pneuma*) mean both 'wind' and 'breath'.

There's fire, too—another indicator of God's active presence (compare Exodus 3:2; Psalm 104:4; Ezekiel 1:4)—not the terrifying fire of judgment (Luke 3:17), but tongue-shaped flames distributed around each head (v. 3), the fire of the Holy Spirit that the Baptist had promised (Luke 3:16). The thing about a flame is that the more you divide it, the more there is to go round: split a flame in half and you get more, not less. So the coming of the Spirit is a gift of new life to the community, which brings out the individual gifts of each member, a gift that brings God's living word to articulate expression in a host of individual tongues (v. 4).

The word on the street

This is not something you can keep behind closed doors! Jerusalem is packed with pilgrims, jostling through the city's narrow streets and full of the excitement of the festival (v. 5). They come from 'every nation under the sun', and they create a ready-made crowd which 'flows together' (v. 6), drawn magnetically to the confused sound coming from behind the shutters, and hearing, mysteriously, not the Galilean Aramaic you would expect (v. 7), but each person's native language (v. 8). The crowd's words in verse 8 could mean 'in our own dialect', suggesting that what they hear is the many different dialects of Aramaic spoken across the Middle East, but in verse 11 they repeat the exclamation with the word 'tongue'.

The nations listed in 2:9–11 cover a much broader language-range than the Aramaic-speaking East, and it's clear that Luke means us to understand this event as a miracle of language. Quite how it relates to the more common association of the Spirit with 'speaking in tongues' (see 10:46; 19:6; 1 Corinthians 14) is unclear, but modern studies have shown that those present often have the sensation of hearing real languages.

PRAYER

Come, Holy Spirit. Blow away the cobwebs from our minds; blow us out on to the streets, and kindle our hearts with the fire of your love.

'THIS IS THAT'

Who was present in that polyglot crowd? Luke's list of nations (possibly taken from a list of diaspora nations) gives a marvellously cosmopolitan dimension to the revelation of God's Spirit, opening up our geographical horizons and preparing us for a story that is going to take us to the ends of the earth (1:8). It's a list that spans the boundaries of Rome's empire, centred not on Rome but on Jerusalem. At Pentecost, pilgrims pour into Jerusalem from all directions: from the east, from the ancient Jewish exilic communities in the old Persian empire (Parthia, Media, Elam, Mesopotamia: v. 9); from the provinces of Asia Minor and the Black Sea coast in the north; from Egypt and north Africa in the south (v. 10); across the sea from Rome (which marks the furthest western boundary on this map), via Crete; and not forgetting the desert caravans of Arabia (v. 11). At the centre, though, is Judea (v. 9), and it may be the locals who are so notably unimpressed by the miracle of languages that all they hear is a drunken babble (v. 13). Miracles by themselves produce wonder, but not conviction (v. 12): Peter has got some serious explaining to do.

Men of Israel

Despite its cosmopolitan nature, this is a Jewish crowd, a crowd of pilgrims gathered in from the scattered nations of the diaspora to worship at the emotional centrepoint of Jewish life (v. 5)—a symbolic foretaste of the gathering in of the diaspora and ultimately of the Gentiles, but at this stage no more than that. When Peter gets up to speak, he addresses the crowd as 'Men of Judea and all you residents of Jerusalem' (v. 14), addressing particularly the sceptics among the local inhabitants (v. 15) and, as will become clear, all the residents, locals and pilgrims who have been in Jerusalem over the festival period and have witnessed the events of Passover (2:22–23). The argument of his speech is quintessentially Jewish, drawing on techniques of biblical exposition known from the Dead Sea Scrolls, leaning on the Jewish scriptures to explain what is actually happening in front of their eyes. You want to know what this is all about? No, they haven't been at the new wine—it's only nine o'clock in the morning (v. 15). To understand what's going on here, you have to look further than that—look back, in fact, to what God has already promised in scripture.

This is what Joel meant

This style of exegesis, known as *pesher* in the Dead Sea Scrolls, is fundamental to the whole argument of Acts and indeed to the biblical understanding of how scripture works. It starts with 'this' (vv. 14, 16) —with the inbreaking revelation of the living God, active in the most unexpected people and places—and then goes back to scripture to match it up with 'that' (v. 16): God's self-revelation in the past. And that may well involve, as it does here, a radical rereading of the scriptures we thought we knew. In fact, as we shall see, the whole of Acts is a plea to read the Bible in a new way in light of the new things that God is doing in the present. So here in verses 17–21 Peter's quotation from Joel 2:28–32 is subtly reshaped to heighten the theological parallels between Joel's prophecy and the events of Pentecost.

I will pour out my Spirit

Joel's prophecy announces the 'great and glorious day of the Lord' (v. 20), a time of judgment for Israel and the nations, accompanied by signs and portents in earth and sky (Joel 2:30–31). The shock comes in Peter's insistence that the 'last days' are happening *now*. The Pentecostal fire and the sound from heaven (Acts 2:2–3) are two of the signs and portents that Joel prophesied (v. 19)—the first but not the last prophetic 'signs' in Acts (compare 4:30; 5:12; 6:8; 7:36; 15:12). And this babble of prophetic speech, giving speech to the inarticulate, empowering men and women alike, matches wonderfully Joel's vision of an outpouring of God's prophetic Spirit on God's people, an inclusive vision that breaks down the barriers of age, class and gender (vv. 17–18). In its original setting, however, Joel's prophecy was about the restoration of Judah and Jerusalem and judgment for the nations of the world (Joel 3:1–8), so Peter's audience (and Peter himself) would not necessarily hear a promise of universal salvation in Acts 2:21 (as Paul does in Romans 10:12–13). The significance of that particular bit of rereading will unfold gradually as Peter's journey takes him out into God's world.

PRAYER

Father, help us to be open to the surprise and challenge of seeing your word fulfilled in ways that explode our narrow horizons.

6

ACTS 2:22–32

'THIS JESUS'

Peter's speech begins with his own and his friends' experience of God's inrushing, overwhelming presence (2:15–16): that's what has pushed them out on to the street, and that's what has attracted the attention of the passers-by (2:1–5). But his priority as an apostle (and the priority of any church that claims to be apostolic) is to redirect that attention from the emissary to the one who sent him, from the gift to the Giver. So here Peter wastes no time in linking the community's experience to the person of Christ (v. 22): Jesus is the interpretive key to everything that happens in Acts.

This Jesus whom you crucified

That also means tying the new events in with a shared recent experience of the audience. Jesus of Nazareth is someone they will all have heard of, and many of them will have seen him preaching and teaching in street and temple in that last week before his death, only seven weeks ago (Luke 19—22). He was a public figure: Peter can assume that his audience will all know of the amazing things God did through Jesus right in their midst (v. 22). So it is clear that Peter is now addressing a very particular audience on a very particular occasion. Acts gives no warrant for the disastrous tendency to blame all Jews everywhere for the death of Jesus, which has blighted Christian history and contributed eventually to the Holocaust. When Peter speaks of 'this Jesus whom you crucified' (vv. 23, 36), he means precisely *this* Jerusalem crowd, the crowd who were part of a very specific series of events just a few weeks before. This is the hard part, but this audience has to face it. We can't move forward into God's future without facing up to our past.

The Jesus whom God raised up

The place of greatest shame and failure, humanly speaking, is the place where God's grace breaks in and transforms the situation. Even at the lowest moment, the moment of the triumph of human sin and failure—the power-plays of the politicians, the fickleness of the crowd, the cowardice of the disciples—even then, Jesus was never outside God's plan (v. 23). Sometimes God allows human action to

32

create a disaster. The crucifixion is about God's passivity, about God in the person of Jesus accepting the worst that humans can do to one another. To suffer is to allow oneself to become an object, to be acted upon: the same Greek word gives us both 'passive' and 'passion'. But that is never the end of the story, because what God does (even in the passive) is always the action of love, and the next event is pure grace (v. 24): resurrection, life that cannot be defeated by death.

David the prophet

Now this whole complex of events, the key to the whole story of Acts, has to be located in scripture and related to the preconceptions of the audience (both Peter's audience and Luke's) about how God acts in the world. The quotation from Psalm 16:8–11 (in vv. 25–28) forms part of a series of classic proof-texts that runs through the sermons and speeches in Acts and, in total, summarizes the key points in the Jewish-Christian debate over the next 200 years. The Psalms play a key role in this debate (see Luke 20:42; 24:44; Acts 1:20; 13:33), especially the psalms (like this one) where the tradition names David as the speaker. Psalm 16 is a great outpouring of hope and faith in the God who sustains his anointed king, and one of the few Old Testament passages that clearly looks forward to a future hope. Ancient interpreters liked to fit the words of the Psalms into the events of David's life, but here David is looking beyond the horizon of the grave to a hope which was not fulfilled in his own lifetime (vv. 26–27).

Taking the words of the psalm literally, Peter points out that when David died, his flesh was subject to the normal processes of bodily decay. The tomb of David is visible proof that he died and was buried in the normal fashion (v. 29). But the words of a prophet cannot be untrue (v. 30), so David must have been referring to somebody else, his divinely appointed descendant (vv. 30–31). Easter proves that Jesus is the Messiah, the anointed successor to David (v. 36). But proof-texts are no good without proof-people: the real witness to the resurrection is its effect in the lives of Peter and his friends (v. 32).

PRAYER

Father, give us the courage to face up to our past and to move forward into your future.

7

GETTING THROUGH

At Catterick Camp there's a poignant painting from World War I showing a young signaller 'lying dead in no-man's land. He had been sent to repair a cable broken down by shellfire. There he lies, cold in death, but with his task accomplished: for beside him lies the rejoined section of cable. Beneath the picture stands one pregnant word—THROUGH.' (Jackson & Wright 1999, p. 23)

The promise of the Father

Now Peter comes back to the Pentecost event. It isn't enough to show that there is a precedent for our spiritual experience in scripture (2:16–21). To understand what is really going on, he has to show how it relates to the central event of all God's self-revelation to the world, to the living key who unlocks the meaning of the whole of scripture (Luke 24:27)—that is, to Jesus himself. So Peter moves seamlessly from resurrection to ascension to Pentecost, from the promise that God's Holy One will be welcomed with joy into the very presence of God (2:28) to the outpouring of the Spirit (v. 33). Only after his death did Jesus win the right to ascend to God's right hand and pour out the Holy Spirit on his followers. Peter last saw Jesus disappearing into a cloud at the top of the Mount of Olives (1:9), and he has only the angels' word to tell him where his Lord has gone. The gift of the Spirit is the proof that Jesus has in fact 'got through' and reconnected the channels of communication between heaven and earth.

Preaching for a result

The effect of Peter's first sermon is electrifying: no scoffers this time! 'What are we to do, brothers?' (v. 37). The question captures the groping confusion that is the prelude to true liberation. In this moment of disorientation, there is a need to hold on to the only people who seem to know their way in this strange new world: the Galileans previously laughed at (2:7, 13) have become 'brothers'. There is a radical shift of perception going on here, a shift of authority and leadership from centre to margins—or, rather, a sudden perception that 'out there' on the margins is the only place we can find salvation.

Peter's hearers also know instinctively that they need something to do, something to seal and solidify the profound changes that are going on in the heart. And that's what Peter goes on to provide, in a fourfold action that has become a pattern for Christian initiation in churches around the world.

Repent and be baptized

Repentance—the basic discipline of admitting 'I was wrong'—is the first and most fundamental response to the challenge of God's word (v. 38). In fact, all the different audiences in Acts are called to repent in one way or another, pagan and Jewish alike (see 3:19; 8:22; 11:18; 17:30; 20:21; 26:20; compare Luke 24:47). This is something that each one in the crowd has to do for themselves, to face up to the challenge of recognizing Jesus as the heart of what God is doing in the world today. But the internal change of heart needs to be accompanied by an external act of public commitment. 'Be baptized in the name of Jesus the Christ,' Peter says: tie your destiny in with his, hitch your waggon to his star.

Forgiveness and the Spirit

From that act of public commitment come the twin benefits of Christian baptism. First, there is the promise of forgiveness, the liberation of the past. For this Jerusalem audience, this means that even the sin of failing to recognize God's Messiah is not unforgivable: it needs to be repented of, like all sin, but there is a way back. Then comes the gift of the Spirit, the liberation of the future. Like John the Baptist in Luke 3:1–18, Peter stands at the threshold of the book of Acts, preaching good news to God's people and reoffering John's baptism—but with a difference: the gift is now on offer to all, just as the prophets had said. Peter's final words glance back at Joel 2:32, and open up wider horizons with the link to Isaiah 57:19. But for now, the important message for Peter's audience is, 'It's for you!'

REFLECTION

'Without forgiveness and reconciliation there can be no future. It is this that lies beneath the hurt and anger of our memories that invade the present, hindering us from moving forward.'

Stuart Ware

8

The CHURCH BEGINS *to* GROW

The day of Pentecost is the birthday of the Church—not of any particular church, but of the one worldwide Church, the glorious fellowship of all who are baptized into the name of Christ. So this chapter ends, fittingly, with a cameo portrait of what being church means, looking back to that momentous day when it all began and forward to the whole yet-to-be-written story of the Church down the ages.

Growth and perseverance

The offer is on the table, but there's a choice to be made, and, although plenty do respond (vv. 41, 47), there's always the possibility that some will not accept it. The task of exhortation is never complete (v. 40). Perseverance is mentioned twice in the Greek text (vv. 42, 46), and it is going to be essential for these new Christians—so new that there isn't even a name for what they've joined. But baptism is the beginning of a new lifestyle, and Luke gives us here the four pillars that mark out and nourish that lifestyle (v. 42).

• **The teaching of the apostles:** The new disciples will need to learn from the Twelve what they had learnt from being with Jesus (1:21–22) and what Jesus had entrusted to them in those 40 precious days between Easter and ascension (Luke 24:44–49; Acts 1:3–4). This is the foundation for the Christian life, and there is no substitute for it. It also means keeping up the habit of discipleship, realizing that students never stop learning—not just from the words of their teachers, but from their actions as well.

• **The fellowship:** Students learn from each other just as much as from their teachers. Being a Christian is about acquiring a new allegiance, following a new Lord, but that is not just a private matter between ourselves and God. There is also a horizontal aspect to this new allegiance: whether we like it or not, we are part of something bigger. We are setting out on the journey with a band of fellow pilgrims—and we're there to sustain and support each other, just as Frodo's companions supported him in Tolkien's *Lord of the Rings*. Trying to be a Christian on our own is asking for trouble.

- **The breaking of bread:** In Paul's letter to the Corinthians, 'breaking bread' together is the quintessential expression of Christian fellowship, a practical way of building community and an act of remembrance of Jesus' death (1 Corinthians 10:16–17; 11:20–34). 'Breaking bread' is clearly something distinct from 'taking nourishment' (v. 46), although both happen together in believers' homes, and both are expressions of Christian fellowship.

- **The prayers:** The church's regular life of prayer (v. 42) continues as the ground-bass behind all these early chapters, something that goes on all the time even though we only occasionally get a glimpse of it (compare 4:24–31). As we see in the next chapter, the temple is the natural place to go to pray (3:1), the focus for the worshipping life of all God's people. There are also set hours for prayer, times when all God's people will be setting aside 'time to be holy'—something that Luke expects his readers to appreciate (since he doesn't bother to explain) as the standard pattern of the spiritual life.

Fellowship in action

The result of all this is, literally, awesome. 'Fear' in Acts (v. 43) is the right and proper reaction to the presence of the living God. That presence continues to be experienced in 'signs and wonders' that embody the life-transforming power of God's kingdom: we shall see an example in the next chapter. It is lived out in the life of the community too, a life that takes 'sharing' seriously (vv. 44–45). The Greek words translated 'possessions and goods' here imply that Luke is talking about disposable property rather than personal homes and possessions. This is practical charity in action, ensuring that no one in the community is needy, rather than the monastic surrender of personal property which was practised at Qumran (see further comment on 4:32–35). The overwhelming impression that comes across from this first phase of the church's existence is grace (v. 47): a lifestyle characterized by 'rejoicing and simplicity of heart' (v. 46), overflowing in praise to God; a community of grace, at peace with itself and thus enjoying the grace and favour of the wider community. It's no wonder that people kept wanting to join them!

PRAYER

Father, keep us faithful in the teaching of the apostles, and help us to live out your grace in the world.

9

LAME MAN LEAPING

Luke's storytelling alternates between 'telling' and 'showing', so Acts contains a series of 'summaries' that tell us what's happening in the church, interspersed with big setpiece 'scenes' that show particular actions in a much more dramatic fashion. Here, in the first big action scene after Pentecost, Luke shows us a specific example of two individual apostles, Peter and John, acting out in their lives some of the general features of the apostolic life. We shouldn't suppose that these were the only examples; Luke selects this story as a typical example of the general pattern of what life was like in those early days after the coming of the Spirit.

Signs and wonders

Peter and John's visit to the temple (v. 1) is part of a standard pattern, a discipline of observing regular times for prayer, but what happens on this particular afternoon is anything but standard. The lame man (v. 2) is also on his regular route, being carried (as he was every day) to a profitable spot for begging, ready to catch the worshippers on their way into the temple. Two paths intersect in an apparently chance encounter, and two sets of lives are changed for ever. Luke's whole tone in this story conveys a sense of breathless awe (v. 10) as we see the first clear demonstration that the apostles now, since the coming of the Spirit, have the same miraculous healing power that Jesus had.

Taking a proper look

Peter looks intently at the lame man, then gets the man to look him in the eye (v. 4). That's what turns a routine, embarrassed transaction, avoiding eye-contact, into a place of real encounter. As it happens, the apostles don't have the silver and gold that the lame beggar wants (v. 5). They have only one thing to offer, and only in the name of Jesus Christ of Nazareth (compare v. 12). The apostles don't wield any kind of miraculous power in their own right, only as agents of Jesus Christ. So the beggar doesn't get what he wanted, but he does get something better. The word Luke uses for 'almsgiving' is the standard Jewish-Greek term *eleemosune*, 'mercy', which perhaps here turns out to be truer than anyone expected. Peter gives the man a hand to raise him up

(v. 7: the same word that the New Testament uses for resurrection). The result is new life, coursing through feet and ankles wobbly from disuse—a dramatic and visible sign of the effects of an encounter with the living God.

Awe and wonder

The healing of the lame man is visible for all to see, and has a dramatic effect on the crowd (vv. 9–10): they are stunned and amazed. This is the correct and expected reaction to seeing the divine life in action, a sense of numinous awe. But this dramatic effect is never an end in itself in Acts: awe and wonder have to be channelled; the sensational has to be put in its theological framework. So the swirling crowd comes to a halt around the centre of the dust-storm, where the once-lame man is holding desperately on to the only people who can help him make sense of the bewilderment and confusion of his new life (v. 11).

In the name of Jesus

This gives Peter his second opportunity for an unscripted sermon (v. 12). His first priority is to direct their focused attention ('Why are you staring at us?') to its proper goal. The miracle was not due to some special power or piety on our part, he says: it was the action of God himself, the God of the Bible, the God of our shared heritage and history (v. 13). Peter quotes Exodus 3:6 here, and the familiar formula reminds his audience that the God they believe in is a God who acts in history, who comes down to save his people. Putting God at the beginning of the sentence is essential—but the sequence is less expected. It is God's power that has healed the lame man (that's the underlying message), but that power is channelled through God's servant Jesus. The essential message of the apostles throughout Acts is that all the miracles they perform are done only in the name of Jesus and testify to the saving power of faith in his name. The apostolic witness always points to Jesus.

REFLECTION

Jesus said, 'Freely you have received, freely give'
(Matthew 10:8, NIV).

It's Your Call

The word Luke uses in 3:13 (*pais*) can mean both 'child' and 'servant' (like the 'boy' of colonial English), and recalls the mysterious 'suffering servant' of Isaiah 52—53 whom God has glorified. But the servant has to suffer before he can be glorified (Isaiah 52:13–14). The terrifying part of Peter's message is that 'you'—that is, the Jerusalem crowd who were caught up in the collective madness that had seized the city only weeks before—have rejected God's holy and righteous servant (v. 14). Peter's words are painfully ironic. The prince of life, the one whose very name is an agent of physical healing (v. 16), is the very one you killed, he says (v. 15). It's a shocking indictment, but the sermon doesn't end there. Telling people they're sinners is *not* the good news! Facing up to what we do to God when he comes among us is not the end of the story, by any means. In fact, it's only the beginning.

Who's to blame?

There are several ways, of course, in which we can evade the indictment: 'We didn't know' is always a good one, or 'We were only obeying orders'. The people of Jerusalem acted in ignorance, Peter says (v. 17), as did their rulers. Peter will confront the ruling authorities later in this episode; here he is very directly addressing the crowd. So Peter is quite happy to accept both of these excuses. In fact, he even adds another way out: it was God all the time. In the words of Sydney Carter's famous song, 'It was God who made the devil, and the woman, and the man: and there wouldn't be an apple if it wasn't in the plan.' Everything that happened to Jesus, Peter says, was part of God's plan, something already revealed by the prophets (v. 18). Interestingly, however, none of this makes the slightest bit of difference to the question of responsibility: you did it, Peter says; you were there, so you need to turn your life around.

It's easy to claim that we were just caught up in the actions of the crowd, or to blame peer pressure or society or our culture or a particular set of social conditions. But that doesn't absolve us as individuals from taking personal responsibility for our own actions: social psychology may be able to tell us why we behave as we do, but (as any teacher knows) we can't change without accepting responsibility for who we are.

What next?

This might seem unfair if Peter was administering punishment. But in fact, he's much more interested in effecting a positive change. What the people need to do is to repent (literally, a change of mind or heart) and turn to God (a complete change of direction). The future, in other words, is more important than the past. The preaching of the gospel can never stop at inducing guilt, focusing on past failings: it's all about opening ourselves to God's future. Repentance opens up the way to the wiping out of sins (v. 19), and the world-changing results are not only individual but communal. Repentance will unleash showers of blessings (v. 20) and even—oddly enough—the return of the Christ (v. 21). Pentecost is simply a foretaste of the real restoration stored up in heaven when all God's promises will be fulfilled. To treat this speech simply as an indictment of 'the Jews' is to miss the point. Luke is much more concerned with repentance than with guilt.

Free gift—act now!

There is also a note of warning, however: the free offer has to be accepted (v. 23). What Peter is offering is nothing more or less than an invitation to take possession of your whole inheritance: it's all there for you. This is what all God's promises are about; it's what all the prophets were saying (v. 24), including Moses himself (vv. 22–23; compare Deuteronomy 18:15–20). In fact, it goes right back to old father Abraham himself (v. 25). What's happening now is part of the original covenant, God's promise of blessing to all the families of the earth (Genesis 12:3), but you have the choice of accepting or rejecting it (v. 26).

PRAYER

Lord, have mercy on our failures, both corporate and individual.
Help us to recognize the new ways of living in the world opened up
through Jesus Christ our Lord.

11

NONE OTHER NAME

To readers familiar with the stories of the prophets, the next twist in Luke's story will come as no surprise. Prophets proclaim God's word: they get into trouble. The Old Testament is full of such stories, and Luke has already pointed up the moral in his Gospel (Luke 13:33–34). But there is also a familiar political pattern to what happens here. The apostles are proclaiming God's word to the people (v. 1), with the result that the ruling classes start to get worried. The pattern is repeated throughout history, from the Wycliffites in 13th-century England to the liberation theologians of 20th-century Latin America.

Who controls the temple?

In fact, you could say that this whole story is about power and control. It's about who controls the temple. Peter and John treat it as a holy space, a place where anyone can go to pray and where God's healing power can be encountered. But the temple authorities regard it as a space that they police, a place where they have the right to control everything that is said. Jesus had similar problems with the temple authorities (Luke 20:1–8). But this isn't a problem unique to the first-century temple authorities. All religious authorities have the tendency to act like this, inside the church as well as outside. The story is also about who controls teaching (v. 2). The Sadducees were the most theologically conservative group in first-century Judaism. They regarded the popular doctrine of the resurrection as unscriptural (see comment on 23:8), and here they are determined to ensure that it is impossible to teach that kind of doctrine within their holy space. Finally, it's about who controls the people. The way Luke tells the story, it looks suspiciously as if the real reason for the arrest is that Peter and John are teaching the people (v. 1), and the point of throwing them into custody (v. 3) is not so much to punish them as to silence them. The incidental note that it is now evening reminds us how much has been packed into this one day: it was already afternoon when Peter and John set out for the temple in 3:1.

Who's really in control?

Events show that neither the temple authorities nor the Sadducees are really in control. Like seed blown from a dandelion clock, the word of

God has its effect, despite the authorities' attempts at weed control. The contrast in verse 4 is piquant: even the arrest doesn't stop 5000 people believing. That's something to hold on to as events unfold and the massed forces of law and order assemble to confront the apostles.

We should not underestimate the social contrasts implied in verses 5–7. The Sanhedrin was the highest court in the land, the apex of political and religious power in first-century Jerusalem, and, of course, the court that had condemned Jesus in Luke 22:66–71. Their question in verse 7 highlights the real point at issue here: 'In what power or in whose name—that is, in whose authority—did you do this?'

Peter's testimony

It is just at this point, when Peter is faced with the question of his life, that Jesus' promise comes true (Luke 21:12–15). The last time he came to the high priest's house, Peter crumbled into denial at a slave-girl's question (Luke 22:54–62). This time, he can face the high priest himself with a fearless proclamation inspired by the Spirit (v. 8). Peter asks, 'You want to know who has the real power in this situation? I'll tell you: it's not us, and it's not you either. It's the one you tried to destroy, the very same Jesus Christ of Nazareth whom you crucified. It was his name that brought salvation to the powerless (v. 9). The very fact that this man is standing before you whole and sound (v. 10) is proof that Jesus is far from dead, that God has raised him from the dead. And the final proof is that God has already showed us this pattern in his word (v. 11).'

The rejected stone of Psalm 118:22 (another favourite text in early Christian polemic) underlines the dynamic of reversal in God's kingdom, a kingdom in which the powerless, the despised, what the world considers 'nothing', become the key to God's salvation. One way or another, we all have to come back to this point: the crucified Christ is either the ultimate stumbling-block or the cornerstone of our salvation (cf. 1 Corinthians 1:18–25).

REFLECTION

Many Christians feel powerless in face of the overwhelming imbalance of power in our world. Faith in 'the name' often seems ridiculous. Pray for them, and for ourselves, that we may hold on to the faith that God is really in control of our world.

12

BOLDNESS *under* FIRE

Empowered by the Spirit, Peter has found words to convince the crowds in street and temple, but the Sanhedrin is a much harder nut to crack. There is no easy conviction here, but a reluctant and grudging admiration from an élite group of men to whom the Galilean apostles are simply illiterate outsiders with no professional training or status (v. 13). What impresses the council is their *parrhesia* or 'boldness' (NRSV). This should be understood not so much in terms of physical courage (although that is implied) as of intellectual and political integrity. That was what struck the council members about Peter and John—that, and the recognition that they had been with Jesus. To the council members, the events we have been witnessing over the past few chapters were simply a confused rumour of street-level disturbance. It is only now that they make the connection with the crucifixion of a Galilean troublemaker some six weeks earlier.

Control order

Admiration can only go so far. The council is not prepared to face up to the implications of what has happened, despite the undeniable public healing of this very public character, who appears to have been thrown into overnight custody with the apostles (vv. 14, 22). So the real problem for this group is not truth but public relations (v. 16), a problem that affects corporate and political life all over the world. This is precisely where *parrhesia* is a necessary civic virtue, and it includes having the spiritual and intellectual integrity to perceive when the normal civic duty to obey those in authority is overridden by a higher duty (v. 19). Ultimately, when the decision is put in those terms, there is no choice (v. 20). This is what apostolic witness boils down to, in the end: simply doing what you've got to do. The verdict could be counted as some kind of moral victory. The apostles are saved by public opinion and let off with a caution (v. 21). It's still the honeymoon period.

The church at prayer

Reporting back to their friends (v. 23) seems an obvious response but it reflects the need for consolidation (after all, they only left to go to afternoon prayers). The community's response might well have been a cautious reassessment: better keep our heads down. Instead, it's a united recourse to prayer (v. 24). True prayer always begins with who God *is* before focusing on our present needs. So this prayer begins by setting out three facts about God. It starts with a cosmic vision of God which puts everything else in proportion: God is the one who created the heaven, the earth, the sea and everything in them. But God is also the living voice of the Holy Spirit (v. 25), linked to a continuous human history of revelation. Through this history, God enters into relationship with human beings: the Lord of creation is also the God who spoke through the mouth of our father David.

Searching the scriptures

The quotation in verses 25–26 is another in the series of key texts used by the early Christians as they sought prayerfully to understand what was happening in their lives. It comes from Psalm 2, which plays a major role in New Testament reflection on Christ, recognizing the 'this' of immediate experience ('in this very city', v. 27) already fore-shadowed in the 'that' of God's self-revelation in scripture. It's a royal psalm about 'the Lord and his Anointed' (*Messiah* in Hebrew, *Christos* in Greek). The 'kings and rulers' who oppose the king in the psalm are identified with Herod and Pontius Pilate in the passion narrative, joining in unholy alliance with the nations and the people of Israel. There is no mention of Israel in the original Hebrew, but the Greek translation uses the two words *ethne* and *laoi* ('nations and peoples') in parallel. For Luke, the *ethne* are always the Gentiles, and *laos* always means the people of Israel. So the psalm-text legitimates a new vision of the world order in which everyone is briefly united against the Christ—although none of this is outside the divine plan (v. 28).

Here and now

The third element of prayer is relating our story to God's story, so what is happening now to the apostles can be read as part of this wider history. But note what the apostles ask for: not protection, not safety, but more boldness and more signs (vv. 29–30). The response is, literally, earth-shaking (v. 31), an overwhelming affirmation by God's Spirit of the apostolic witness.

PRAYER

Lord Jesus, may our lives reflect the fact that we have been with you.

13 ACTS 4:32–37

EVERYTHING *in* COMMON

Here Luke shows us the power of God's Spirit at work on two fronts simultaneously. On the external, visible front, the apostles continue to exercise their task of public testimony to the resurrection of Jesus. It's a task that they tackle firmly—affirmed by their renewed experience of God's invigorating presence in 4:31—but not aggressively or rudely. Everything is done with 'great grace' (v. 33; compare Colossians 4:6).

Luke also gives us a glimpse behind the scenes into the invisible, internal life of the community (v. 32). It is just as important that the whole inner life of the church and its ordinary, bog-standard members (that's you and me) should also show the power of God's Holy Spirit at work. Otherwise, the testimony of the apostles will be fatally undermined. Luke's picture of the infant church (still in its first weeks of life) is one in which the life of the Spirit is visible in the way Christians relate to each other. This is, in many ways, the most basic function of the Spirit (much more basic than 'gifts'). Paul calls it the *koinonia* or 'fellowship' of the Holy Spirit (2 Corinthians 13:13), and it has profound implications for the way Christians are called to live out their lives together in the actual realities of congregational life (see Philippians 2:1–5).

Koinonia in action

Luke has already described one very practical outworking of *koinonia*: it means that Christians hold everything in common (*koina*) for the relief of those in need (2:44), and here he returns to the theme (v. 32). Luke's language here evokes the ideal picture of the wilderness community in Deuteronomy 15:4–11 (and might also remind some of his readers of the Greek philosophers' vision of a utopian community where all property was held in common for the good of all). We know that the Qumran community operated some form of monastic pooling of property, and this provides corroboration that such practices were part of the world of the early church. But Luke probably doesn't mean an early form of communism so much as a willingness to put everything at the disposal of others. Believers held their private property as a trust to be used by God.

The details become clearer in verse 34: those who could afford it sold their possessions as need arose, and what people sold was not their own homes but any disposable property that they happened to have (2:46

and 12:12 make it clear that believers still kept their own homes). The object is not to disadvantage themselves but to use their surplus assets to raise money for those in need. The apostles thus find themselves acting as middlemen in a sort of ad hoc centralized distribution system, which will soon become too much (see ch. 6). But already there is a suggestion that the numbers in the church have grown since 2:45, when the distribution to needy members of the community happened directly without involving the apostles. (See comment on 2:44–45.)

The son of consolation

Moving from the general to the particular, Barnabas enters the story (vv. 36–37) simply as a positive, concrete example of the general picture that Luke is painting. This is an affectionate portrait of one of Luke's most attractive characters, one who is going to provide an important link between Jerusalem and Antioch (11:25–26), and between the Jerusalem apostles and Paul (9:27). The tribe of Levi, which performed certain liturgical duties in the temple, was not supposed to own property within Israel (Deuteronomy 10:9), which probably means that the farm Barnabas sold was in Cyprus (v. 37).

The *koinonia* challenge

It's easy to dismiss Luke's picture of the early church as utopian. The fact is, however, that the interactive social care practised by the early churches for their poorer members made a huge impression on outsiders and played a vital part in the mission and survival of the church in the early centuries. As late as the second century, the satirical Greek writer Lucian notes that Christians in Syria believed in holding their property in common (Lucian, *Peregrinus* 13). It's an idea that rather frightens us in the affluent West today, and it's worth wondering why; but it is a fact that sitting light to personal property and seeking to resist the tyranny of the acquisitive society has always lain close to the surface for those who seek to follow Jesus. (Luke's Gospel has some pretty tough things to say about personal wealth, too: see Luke 1:53; 3:11; 6:24–25; 12:13–24; 16:19–31; 18:18–30).

REFLECTION

'I can't hear your words because your actions are shouting too loud!'
All too often it's the inner, private behaviour of Christians towards
one another that prevents people from hearing the gospel message.

14

LIVING *in an* OPEN UNIVERSE

What is it about money that brings out our worst instincts? Following on from the description of the 'community of goods' in 4:32–34, Ananias and Sapphira provide a negative counterweight to the positive example of Barnabas (4:36–37). Maybe, as astute businesspeople, they thought they could put one over on the gullible Galilean apostles, with their naïve ideas about sharing property. Whatever way you look at it, this is a most uncomfortable story, and it raises two kinds of question.

Does it make historical sense?

Many readers wonder what all the fuss is about. What exactly was the process that Luke is describing? What did Ananias and Sapphira do wrong? There are irresistible parallels with the Qumran community, where new members were expected to put their whole property at the community's disposal. But that doesn't seem to be quite what Luke is describing here: Peter stresses that the gift is voluntary (v. 4). Ananias and Sapphira were quite free to disagree with the principle of *koinonia*, or to withhold any amount of their own property that they liked.

The language of verse 2 provides a better clue to the cultural framework of the story. The rare word *enosphisato* ('kept back', NRSV) recalls the story of Achan in Joshua 7, where it is used of embezzling funds placed in sacred trust. The same word turns up in 2 Maccabees 4:32, in a story designed to show the numinous, supernatural power invested in a holy place which is under threat. For Luke, this is a story about the holiness of the *ecclesia* (v. 11). This primitive *koinonia*, which doesn't even have a building of its own to meet in, is the dwelling-place of God's Holy Spirit and has the same kind of scary holiness as the temple itself (compare 1 Corinthians 3:16–17).

Does it make moral sense?

We can begin to see why the story had a point for Luke's first readers. Luke is talking about a tiny, persecuted church, and the message of the story is both an encouragement to its members and a warning to anyone who tries to mess with it. God does care what happens to this apparently insignificant group. Most of us still find it morally repugnant now: the death penalty seems a bit extreme for anyone embezzling church funds. But it's worth pondering the underlying significance of the story. What Luke gives us here is a dramatized representation of an important truth about the integrity of the church. The church is more than the human institution we see, with all its human foibles and failings. It's the dwelling of God's Holy Spirit: like Moses at the burning bush (Exodus 3:6), we stand on holy ground, and on that ground nothing less than utter truthfulness will do. Nothing destroys community quicker than equivocation in interpersonal relations. It is not disagreement that destroys Christian community so much as a failure to acknowledge the truth before each other and before God's Holy Spirit (vv. 3–4, 9).

Danger—God at work

Fear (v. 11) is a natural reaction to these events. In the world of the Bible, fear—or, perhaps better, awe—is seen as a wholly appropriate reaction to the visible manifestation of God at work. We should note that it is not our job to induce fear by hellfire preaching or puritanical discipline, but where God is at work there is a sense in which the right and proper response is one of awe, mingled with a rather wary and distant respect (v. 13).

Nevertheless, people are still joining the church, which is now so large that it has taken over one of the city's public spaces (v. 12). The sense of awe that God is at work here in an extraordinary way is reinforced by the healing power displayed by the apostles, especially Peter (vv. 15–16). God has answered the apostles' prayer in 4:29–30 in a dramatic and incontrovertible way. This is part of the proof that Jesus is not dead: his Spirit is carrying on his healing ministry in the work of his church. An apostolic church is a church in which God is visibly at work, a church carrying on the mission of Jesus and empowered by the life of his Spirit.

REFLECTION

'If then our common life in Christ yields anything to stir the heart, any loving consolation, any sharing of the Spirit, any warmth of affection or compassion, fill up my cup of happiness by thinking and feeling alike, with… a common care for unity' (Philippians 2:1–2, NEB). How does 'the fellowship of the Spirit' actually show itself in our life together as Christians?

15

WE MUST OBEY GOD

In this scene we glimpse another side of the apostolic persona. The apostles have real authority, real spiritual power, but real vulnerability and pain too. 'You have stood by me in my trials,' said Jesus in Luke 22:28, and here we see a Peter who has learned from his failures, who has now been 'strengthened' so that he can strengthen his brothers by example (Luke 22:32). As Latin American theologian Justo Gonzalez remarks (2001, pp. 86ff.), the preaching of marginality sounds rather different to poor churches who are already marginalized. They need to hear the underlying message of strength and hope in the living God.

A hand on the shoulder

The church is winning popular support (5:13), but predictably the authorities are going to be less pleased (v. 17). The group is growing in size, attracting huge crowds to its public meetings in the temple. The right to free speech and public association only goes so far, even in a modern democracy: sooner or later, you're going to be 'moved on'. The authorities' motives are not necessarily bad in themselves. 'Zeal' (v. 17: NRSV 'jealousy') can be a positive thing (see comment on 13:45 and 17:5), but, from Luke's point of view, it's misdirected. The tragedy in this story is that both sides believe they are doing God's will. For Luke and his readers, though, there is no room for doubt: the angel's message (vv. 19–21) makes it quite clear that preaching the 'words of this life' in the temple is precisely what the apostles ought to be doing.

The great escape

Luke's gift for dramatic irony is evident in this scene, which is not without a touch of slapstick humour. The council convenes in all its official splendour (v. 21), only to discover that the jail is empty (vv. 22–23). Luke's carefully drawn picture, with all the different elements precisely described, brings out the irony of a situation in which the powerful, those in control of the judiciary and all the vested interests of church and state (the Establishment, if you like), find out that they are not in control at all. In fact, they are completely at a loss (v. 24). Meanwhile, the powerless—those who have no resources except their own integrity and their obedience to God—have escaped from prison and are unconcernedly pursuing their God-given task of 'teaching the people' (v. 25), who have a much better instinct than their leaders for where the real authority lies (v. 26).

Civil disobedience

The humour underlines dramatically the real issue that Luke is highlighting in this episode. The apostles have embarked on a campaign of civil disobedience: they have knowingly ignored a court injunction imposed by the legally constituted judicial authority of their country. Thus far, the court has right (as well as might) on its side. This was a situation often experienced by Jews seeking to remain faithful to their religious identity in a world where secular power was held by the pagan empires. Daniel 6 provides the classic template. Like Daniel, the apostles have only one defence: that the legal duty of all law-abiding citizens to obey the courts is overridden by a higher duty to obey God. This is a dangerous claim (and Luke is no political radical), but everything in this narrative—the miracle of the escape, the angel, the power of the apostles' preaching, the testimony of the Holy Spirit (v. 32)—bears out their words. Luke's message is that God is not on the side of the big battalions. As the prophet Elisha said to his petrified servant Gehazi, 'There are more with us than there are with them' (2 Kings 6:16).

How do you tell?

Apostles also need the gifts of wisdom and discernment, however. It takes an enormous amount of courage and faith in a real-life situation to hold on to the apostles' perception. Standing up against the forces of law and order—even against the spiritual leaders of one's own people—does not come easily to naturally law-abiding citizens. It takes perception to see when the forces of law and order have been subverted and must be resisted in God's name. The apostles' words in verse 29 appear on the tomb of Cardinal-Archbishop Galen of Munster, one of the very few churchmen to resist openly the growing domination of Nazism in German political life in the 1930s, and they have inspired many Christians (and others) in the courageous decision to say 'No' to a corrupt exercise of power.

PRAYER

Father, give us the humility to obey, the courage to resist,
and the wisdom to know the difference.

DARE *to* BE *a* GAMALIEL

Luke now draws us into an unusual behind-the-scenes peep into the council's private deliberations, thus giving us the chance to exercise a bit of empathy by looking at the whole sequence of events from the point of view of the authorities.

Behind closed doors

Inside this slightly farcical narrative is a surprisingly sympathetic dramatization of the real dilemma facing the council—the same dilemma that faces anyone called to a position of authority in church or state. Yes, it takes courage to 'dare to be a Daniel', but it's too easy to assume that Daniel is always right. Look at Romans 13 for a powerful exposition of the classic view that the authority of the state (even the pagan state) is God-given and must be respected. 'Pray for the peace of the government,' said the later rabbis, 'for without it, we would have eaten one another alive.'

The problem of Theudas

Gamaliel was one of the great Pharisaic sages of his day, and a man deeply respected for his wisdom and integrity. But there is a real problem about taking this passage as a transcript of an actual speech. Theudas (v. 36) was a real historical figure, mentioned by the contemporary Jewish historian Josephus alongside Judas the Galilean (Josephus, *Antiquities*, 20.97–98). Judas (v. 37) was the ringleader in the first stirrings of Jewish revolt against the Romans at the time of the census in AD6, but Theudas was active in the 40s, a decade after the dramatic date of Gamaliel's speech. Josephus mentions Theudas and Judas in the same paragraph and in the same order as Gamaliel does—which is odd, because it is the reverse of the historical order.

The problem of the speeches

More generally, this passage illustrates the historical problem of the speeches in Acts. It's clear that they cannot automatically be treated as actual transcripts of the words spoken on any given occasion (especially in Jerusalem). There are really two possibilities: either they are totally fictitious (Luke made up the occasion and the words), or the occasion is genuine and Luke gives the gist of the argument but adds circumstantial detail of his own. The latter would be in line with the normal practice of ancient historians like Thucydides. Either way, it is important to remember that Luke's speeches are written *post factum* and serve a rhetorical function, addressing Luke's own readers as much as the dramatic audience in the story. In other words, Luke is telling this story not just to explain what happened in the past, but as a part of an active debate that is still going on.

Don't fight with God

The real point about this speech is the theological warning that it gives to Luke's readers, then and now. For his first readers, the message is, 'Beware! Watch what you're doing' (v. 36). There is still a real decision to be made about this 'new thing': the nation's future hangs on a knife-edge. This, in many ways, is the underlying question of the whole of Acts: what's going on, and is it of God? (v. 38). Any reader familiar with the Jewish scriptures would be able to bring to mind prophetic warnings that were heeded or not heeded, and Gamaliel's message is just as relevant to the church today. The Gamaliel principle can be dangerous if it becomes a way of avoiding making decisions and allowing injustice to continue unchecked (Gonzalez 2001, p. 85), but in many ways his question is the real question we need to be asking ourselves when any 'new thing' threatens our security, our comfortable patterns of faith and worship. Where is God in all this? Is God here with us, cowering behind the bastions of 'what we've always done'? Or is God out there too, nudging and surprising us into new ways of seeing the world? It needs faith, discernment, and the ability to wait humbly on God.

PRAYER

In a world of change, Father, thank you for your unchanging truth.
Help us to meet you both in the stability of tradition and in the
excitement of change.

17

ACTS 6:1–4

HEBREWS & HELLENISTS

Chapter 6 marks a transition to the next phase of the church's life, a phase that will see the apostles, and the church, begin to broaden their horizons in unexpected ways. It begins (as so often) with a problem—a church beset by a groundswell of grumbling (v. 1) that finally reaches the ears of the apostles. In such a situation, it's often helpful to do a SWOT analysis: what are the strengths, weaknesses, opportunities and threats for this church?

Strengths

It is, of course, a nice problem to have—a problem caused by the church's continual growth in numbers (v. 1). We don't know exactly when this growth happened, but we must assume that God has continued to add to the church daily those who are being saved (2:47), and we must be looking now at a church numbering several thousands. Moreover, it is an increasingly varied congregation, drawing on the two main groupings of the Jewish community in Jerusalem: the 'Hebrews' (Aramaic-speaking Jews) and the 'Hellenists' (Greek-speaking Jews). It is also a strength that the disciples have continued their commitment to pooling their surplus assets and dispensing charity to the needy.

Weaknesses

Size creates its own problems, however. The church has begun to outgrow its original structures, and the old, individual sense of being in a community where everyone matters is getting lost. This is partly a matter of administrative systems. What worked for a group of 120 (1:15) would hardly work for a group of over 5000 (2:41; 4:4), without any central building or paid administration. The simple and expressive act of laying contributions at the apostles' feet (4:35–37) is placing an intolerable burden of administration on the apostles: no wonder some people are feeling overlooked! And it sounds as if the multicultural variety within the body of believers is also creating its own problems, with the language of 'us' and 'them' and 'it's not fair' creeping in. Was there also a sense that the original believers had become some kind of 'in group', with the newer converts feeling left out? Did the older church members feel threatened by these brash new arrivals? What had they done to integrate the newcomers and make them feel welcome?

Opportunities

There is always a temptation for church leaders to treat 'grumbling' as a threat to their own authority, but the apostles treat it as an opportunity to listen to what God is saying to them in this situation (v. 2). When someone says to us, 'You're doing too much', it's easy to feel defensive about 'my ministry' (look at Moses in Exodus 18), but actually it's an opportunity to take stock, and to realize that God has other people out there who have gifts and ministries too. So we see the first indications here that being an apostle is only one of a variety of ministries within the whole body (1 Corinthians 12; Ephesians 4). The apostles spot not only the opportunity to delegate (v. 3) but the opportunity to decentralize, resisting the temptation to keep all forms of power, financial as well as spiritual, in their own hands. That, of course, creates opportunities for other people to act as benefactors, to have the joy of ministering to people's needs, to realize that they too can be filled with God's Spirit and have a ministry to fulfil.

Threats

One person's opportunity is another person's threat! Multiculturalism —even growth, the arrival of new faces—can be seen as a threat by some communities. Collaborative ministry and the need to recognize the gifts of others can be a threat to many church leaders. And it isn't only leaders who suffer from this problem. Church members too can feel threatened by the gifts of others, and spend their time trying to denigrate them (look again at 1 Corinthians 12). Equally, though, church members can feel threatened by leaders who treat them as autonomous adults and say, 'Here's the problem—you sort it out' (v. 3). Peter and the apostles are effectively treating the body of believers here like a civic assembly, saying, 'This isn't our church—it's yours too, and it's just as much your responsibility as ours to be open to the Spirit's guidance and responsive to the needs of the world.'

PRAYER

Father, help us to see opportunities for you in place of threats, and to call on your strength in our weakness.

A DEACON *in* DANGER

The election of Stephen and his fellow deacons is like dislodging a pebble on a mountain path and triggering a landslide—a small action, but one with enormous consequences for the narrative of Acts and for the history of the church. It's amazing what happens when you trust the Spirit!

Varieties of service

The gift of the Spirit isn't just for the visible, up-front tasks in the life of the church: backroom administration and balancing the books need prayer too. In fact, this story isn't so much about delegation as about trust. The apostles have to trust the people—trust their choice, and trust that there are others out there already 'full of the Spirit'. Both apostles and people then have to trust the Spirit, trust that the Spirit will continue to call and empower people for service in God's church. This is not 'top-down' management—or, rather, the apostles are not the ones at the top!

Luke never actually calls the Seven 'deacons'—all who serve in God's church are engaged in *diakonia* (ministry) of one kind or another (6:4)—but the word *diakonia* came to be used especially of practical service to the local congregation, in which the administration of charity was always important. Since that implies the identification of local needs, deacons came to be assigned a special role (which they still have in the Orthodox churches) of presenting the offerings of the people and voicing their prayers.

The laying on of hands

This scene also gives us the prototype for the ordination of ministers for specific service in God's church. Note that Stephen and his colleagues already have the gift of the Spirit (6:3); the laying on of hands (v. 6) is both a confirmation of the gift and a commissioning for a new task. Discerning someone else's vocation is always a risky but exciting task, calling for sensitivity to what God is already doing, and lots of prayer.

The result for the Jerusalem church surpasses all expectations, with the growth pattern apparently unstoppable (v. 7). Most of the group ordained as 'deacons' here disappear from Luke's story after this chapter, but Philip and Stephen are going to be very important in the next few chapters, and they quickly grow out of the limited role originally assigned to them (v. 8). That little spot of 'grumbling' (6:1), along with the apostles' willingness to extend their ministry, has unwittingly (and under the guidance of God's Spirit) brought two new players on to the scene.

Stephen the Hellenist

Who was Stephen? It seems clear that he was one of the 'Hellenists' of 6:1. His name is Greek (it means 'crown'), as are all the names in verse 5, and he has his own personal network in the Greek-speaking synagogues of diaspora Jews settled in Jerusalem (v. 9). It is not quite clear how many congregations Luke is talking about here, but they come from all the great cities of the empire. Alexandria, Tarsus (Cilicia) and Ephesus (Asia) are all known to have had major Jewish communities, and Rome is where the 'Libertini' (a Latin term meaning 'freed slaves') came from. The gospel is starting to engage in conversation with new dialogue partners—a small but highly influential grouping in Jerusalem, and one which is going to play an increasingly important role in Acts. This group has a strong theological commitment to the Law of Moses, which is the most important badge of identity for Jews living in pagan countries (v. 11), but it also has wider horizons and a broader vision of God's scattered people.

Stephen the disciple

The most important thing about Stephen, for Luke, is that he is full of the Spirit (v. 5). Someone who had (probably) never met Jesus in person finds Jesus' words in Luke 21:15 a living reality in his life: no one is able to withstand his wisdom and Spirit (v. 10). Like the apostles, he finds very quickly that the call to follow Jesus leads him into violent confrontation (v. 12), and from there into direct imitation of his Lord in suffering and death. The stage is set for a dramatic confrontation.

FOR REFLECTION AND PRAYER

'There are varieties of service, but the same Lord' (1 Corinthians 12:5). Whatever the service we are called to, help us to remember that we are gifted by the same Spirit and serve the same Lord.

19 ACTS 7:1–16

A VISION & a PROMISE

Stephen's speech is the longest in the book of Acts, and introduces a new set of themes. It continues the apologetic started by Peter, but in a different style, retelling the Bible story rather than appealing to proof-texts and drawing on different scriptures. At first sight, it seems to have little relevance to the charge of speaking 'against this holy place and the law' (6:13–14), but in fact it is highly pertinent. Stephen focuses on texts from the Law of Moses (the first five books of the Hebrew scriptures), on the figure of Moses himself, and (right at the end of the speech) on 'this place'—that is, the temple. In effect, what Stephen is doing is to undercut the charge of abandoning the Mosaic Law by appealing to a higher authority.

The vision

What Stephen gives his audience (and what Luke gives his readers in this speech) is a whistlestop tour of the whole of biblical history, from Abraham to Joshua. But the significance lies in what he selects and what he leaves out. It is a powerful retelling of Israel's past, addressed to people who share that past ('brothers and fathers', v. 2) but re-aligned to recall them to their roots. Stephen begins with Abraham, the starting point of Israel's experience of the living God, which is also the beginning of Israel's existence as a people (Genesis 12:1; compare Hebrews 11:8–12). Right from the start, it's a story that has the God of glory as its subject (v. 2). Following the Greek translation of the Bible, Stephen rephrases the call of Abraham into the language of vision—a constant theme in Acts. Behind the condensed storyline (vv. 3–5) lies careful study of the complicated story of Abram's call in Genesis 11:31—12:9, a two-stage process that adds up to a single experience of God's calling (Genesis 15:7).

The promise

God's call is to 'come out' (v. 3). It's all about leaving present certainties and committing ourselves to an uncertain future—but a future with God in it. But what is Abraham called to come out to? Stephen's potted history emphasizes the coming out more than the eventual destination, the letting go of certainties more than the acquisition of new possessions. The land to which Abraham was called is the land that we (Stephen reminds his audience) are now living in (v. 4), but Abraham was not given so much as a foot's length in it. The promise was not for him but for his descendants (v. 5, literally 'seed')—a seed that didn't even exist when the promise was made. Before coming into the promised inheritance, Abraham's progeny would have to endure exile and slavery (v. 6). The covenant looked ahead to the exodus (v. 7), focusing not so much on the promised land (Genesis 15:18–21) as on the creation of a worshipping people (Exodus 3:12; compare Luke 1:74). Circumcision (v. 8) was especially important as an identity marker to diaspora communities: Stephen reminds his hearers that it is part of the covenant with Abraham, not the Law of Moses.

A feuding family

Stephen assumes a basic knowledge of the patriarchal narratives (v. 8), but focuses on the part of the story closest to diaspora experience. Joseph (v. 9) was (like Daniel and Esther) a prototype diaspora hero, prospering in exile and bringing salvation both to his host country and to his own people. But this part of the story also highlights the long history of fratricidal feuding within the patriarchal family. Stephen reminds his audience that the history of God's people is a history of jealousy and rejection within the family, a story of exclusion and betrayal. So Joseph becomes a kind of prototype for Jesus himself, rejected by his brothers but honoured by outsiders because God is with him (v. 10; compare Genesis 39:2), and God enables him to become a saviour to his own people (vv. 11–14; compare Genesis 45:7–8). The final summary brings the Genesis story down to the death of Jacob and his sons (v. 15) and their burial in Shechem (v. 16)—a detail which seems to be a confusion of two burial stories in Genesis (compare Genesis 23:15; 33:19; 50:13; Joshua 24:32).

PRAYER

Father, give us the faith of Abraham, to leave behind our comfortable certainties and journey out with you in obedience and trust.

20 ACTS 7:17-34

ISRAEL *in* EGYPT

It's all about timing. At the exact moment when all seems lost, God acts to save his people. It's not always easy to recognize God's saving acts, however, when your eyes are blinded by the tears and sweat of struggling with a hostile world.

In the nick of time

Stephen's story moves on to the exodus, to the time of the promise (v. 17). Time is of the essence here as two storylines converge: the prolonged sojourn of Jacob's descendants in Egypt, and the promise given to Abraham 400 years before. The time of promise is also the time of greatest danger. God had warned of exile and ill-treatment (7:6-7), and the quotation from Exodus 1:9-11 (v. 18) underlines the precariousness of 'diaspora' existence—how much it depends on having somebody at the top of the system who knows you and remembers why you are there. But it's precisely at this time of greatest danger that God sends a saviour for his people (v. 20), a baby whom his parents recognize as beautiful before God (*asteios*).

This whole story is told in words taken from the exodus narrative in the Greek Bible, though with some subtle alterations that focus the narrative on the tiny scrap of life on whom the safety of God's people hangs. Stephen misses out the courage of the midwives (Exodus 1:15-21) and the faith of Moses' mother and sister (Exodus 2:1-4; see Hebrews 11:23), and implies that Moses was being exposed (v. 21), that is, left out to be taken by wild animals or rescued by passers-by. This was a common method of disposing of unwanted babies in Egypt and the Greco-Roman world, and one that Jews and Christians consistently refused to follow. This adds a sobering touch of realism to the well-known story of the baby in the bulrushes, but also a fairytale quality which would not have been lost on Luke's Greek readers. Greek myth and legend were full of tales of babies (like Oedipus) who were exposed at birth and returned in adulthood to claim their rightful inheritance.

The unknown prince

So Moses is brought up in the palace (v. 21), inheriting and surpassing all the wisdom the pagan world could offer (v. 22)—a privileged existence that lasts for 40 years (v. 23). This detail is not in Exodus: Stephen is part of an ongoing Jewish tradition working out the chronology of the whole story (compare v. 30). But Moses' return to claim his place among his own people has a paradoxical quality. As the letter to the Hebrews puts it, for Moses it means a descent from the privileged cocoon of palace life to the harsh realities of life among an oppressed and marginalized people (v. 24; compare Hebrews 11:24–26). In such conditions, the oppressed can easily turn on their fellows, venting their frustration and impotent rage on each other, or on the person trying to help, rather than on the system that causes the oppression (vv. 26–28). Moses has the humiliation of wanting to be recognized as a God-sent agent of salvation (*soteria*), but totally failing to convince the people he is trying to help (v. 25). The question, 'Who sent you?' (v. 27) is deeply ironic, as 7:35 shows; but it is also perhaps a salutary warning to Moses. He has good intentions, a vague idea that something needs to be done, but he hasn't yet been into the desert to discover himself and receive his call (v. 29). He doesn't really know himself who has sent him.

A vision in the desert

Before he can save his people, Moses has to experience the precariousness of *paroikia*, living as an alien, for himself—and also to find himself as a man, a human being, a father. It is all too easy for missionaries (and charities) to come in from outside and offer solutions without knowing what it's like on the ground. But identification is not enough (otherwise the Hebrews could have saved themselves). Moses also needs a vision (v. 30), recalling the foundational vision of Abraham (v. 32) as God calls out his people anew. However well-intentioned our desire to save the world, it will run into the sand unless it is grounded in attentiveness and obedience to what God is doing. God (as always in the Bible) is the real hero of this story, the one who has heard and seen what is happening to his people and is determined to rescue them (v. 34). Before anything else, Moses has to turn aside from his daily work (v. 31) and realize with awe that he stands on holy ground (v. 33).

PRAYER

Father, lead us out into the desert to meet with you face to face.
Then send us back to work for the salvation of your world.

A SAVIOUR REJECTED

It is this encounter with God and obedience to God's call that makes it possible for Moses to go back to Egypt and save his people. He returns to his task as someone sent by God, but that doesn't make life any easier for him.

This Moses

There is a deep irony (underlined in the word order in the Greek) in the fact that it was *this* Moses, the same one whom his people had denied and rebuffed, who was in fact sent and called by God to be their ruler and redeemer (v. 35: 'this one' [*houtos*] comes in an emphatic position five times in verses 35–38). The words Stephen uses deliberately point up the parallel with Jesus, the Saviour sent by God but rejected by his own people. This is the one who has the God-given power to bring his people out of slavery and to perform signs and wonders in the wilderness (v. 36), and it was this same Moses who prophesied that God would raise up another prophet 'like me' (Deuteronomy 18:15). Far from denying the importance of Moses, in other words, Stephen argues that Moses himself pointed forward to God's salvation in Jesus, both in his words and through the paradigm of his life.

The golden calf

From verse 39 onwards, the focus moves from Moses to the people he led, with the emphasis on rejection and a shift from 'us' to 'them'. The pace of the story quickens as Stephen links the events in the wilderness with the ultimate tragedy of exile. The essential seeds of the tragedy are already there in the Exodus narrative of the golden calf (Exodus 32), a story that was a sore point to contemporary Jewish exegesis (Josephus leaves it out altogether in his rewriting of biblical history in *Antiquities* 3.93–102). How could God's redeemed people, at the foot of Mount Sinai itself, indulge in this blatant piece of idolatrous worship? Stephen identifies the fateful steps that led to disaster: disobedience, hankering for the past life (v. 39), loss of confidence in their leader (v. 40), then the making of the golden calf itself (v. 41). Stephen's language highlights the fact that the people had fallen into nothing less than the pagan sin of idolatry (see Exodus 20:4–6).

From idolatry to exile

Finally comes the chilling verdict (v. 42): the people had turned away from God, so God turns away from them and hands them over to the worship of the host of heaven (compare Isaiah 63:10, where the same verb is used). The 'host of heaven' is a reference to the star-gods of neighbouring cultures, a development foreshadowed in Deuteronomy 4:19 and frequently denounced in the later prophets (see, for example, Jeremiah 8:2; Zephaniah 1:5). Stephen is able to link it to the wilderness period through the mysterious text from Amos 5:25–27 which he cites in verses 42–43. This text is hard to interpret even in the Hebrew, and may refer to a tradition (also preserved in Jeremiah 7:21–26) that Israel did not offer animal sacrifices in the wilderness. But Stephen focuses on the word *moi* ('to me') at the end of the first line of the quotation, and implies that the house of Israel did offer sacrifice in the wilderness (as we know from v. 41), but not to the God who had redeemed them.

Rereading the Bible

These verses provide a nice illustration of the way ancient exegetes, both Jewish and Christian, adapted the text of the Bible to their own circumstances. Amos was writing in the eighth century BC, and the Greek translators of the Hebrew scriptures, working some 600 years later, could not understand all the allusions in Amos's rather obscure Hebrew. That's why the text that Stephen quotes is rather different from what we find in an English Old Testament, although the end result is well in accord with Amos' fierce description of the 'day of the Lord' (Amos 5:18–27). The Hebrew *sikkut* in Amos 5:26 was probably the name of an Assyrian god (Sakkut), but in the Greek Bible (and thus also in Acts 7:43) it becomes 'tabernacle' (*sukkat*). The Hebrew *melech*, 'king', is reread with different vowels as Moloch, the name of a pagan deity (compare Jeremiah 39:35). The mysterious Kaiwan (or Raiphan) defeated the ancient scribes completely. The only substantial change in Stephen's quotation, however, is the change from Damascus to Babylon: Syria was the enemy when Amos was writing, but later readers inevitably assimilated the old prophetic warnings to the more famous exile in Babylon.

PRAYER

Father, as we journey with you across the wilderness, keep us mindful of the cost of our salvation and faithful to the one who calls us.

22

YOUR GOD IS TOO SMALL

If the worship of gods made with human hands is idolatry, what of the construction of a sanctuary made with human hands? This seems to be the underlying theme that links the two final sections of Stephen's speech, both almost certainly derived from centuries of reflection and preaching in the synagogue. We can see traces of this debate in the patterns and links made in contemporary Jewish exegesis, both Hellenistic and rabbinic.

From tabernacle to temple

Stephen crashes through the final stages of salvation history very fast: Joshua's conquest of the promised land (v. 45) does not really interest him. What does concern him is the shift between the tabernacle (v. 44), the sign of God's grace to a pilgrim people, and the temple—the more permanent dwelling-place for God that David longed to build and Solomon completed (vv. 46–47; compare Psalm 132:5). His final answer to his accusers picks up again on a well-established biblical theme: the inadequacy of all attempts to pin God down. The passage he quotes from Isaiah 66:1–2 expresses one side of a deep-rooted ambivalence in biblical tradition about the location of worship in the temple, an ambivalence brought out in the story of Nathan (2 Samuel 7) and by Solomon himself (1 Kings 8). It expresses one of the fundamental insights of the book of Acts—that the temptation to idolatry, the temptation of limiting God to inadequate human conceptions of the divine, is prevalent in all human societies, Jewish or pagan.

The parting of the ways

Stephen's final words (vv. 51–53) crackle with the pain of the 'parting of the ways' between church and synagogue. Seen from the other side of that divide, it's a despairing indictment of the failures of God's chosen people to recognize the work of the Holy Spirit, tracing a damning line of rejection from the wilderness generation right through to the sufferings of Israel's prophets—a theme echoed in Luke's Gospel (see Luke 13:33–35; 19:41–44), in Hebrews 11, and in other Jewish and Christian writings of the Second Temple period.

In the early church's apologetic, this prophetic rejection was linked with the prophetic witness to Christ. The rejection of the Holy Spirit who speaks through the prophets thus becomes a way of explaining (or simply expressing) the puzzling fact that the scriptures which, to Christians, self-evidently prophesy the coming of Jesus are read in a very different way by Jewish readers (2 Corinthians 3—4 is another way of expressing this puzzle). The fact is that there is no 'neutral' way of reading the Bible. Throughout their history of mutual incomprehension, Jews and Christians have appealed to the same texts but interpreted them very differently.

Reading after the Holocaust

It is important for us, reading in a post-Holocaust world, to keep a hold on the dramatic setting of Stephen's words. Stephen is addressing the Sanhedrin in Jerusalem within weeks of Jesus' death. In this context his words have a particular sense, and emphasize that his quarrel is not with the Law of Moses but with those who fail to keep it. Many of Stephen's contemporaries at Qumran would have said the same (though for different reasons): the Dead Sea Scrolls contain even more chilling indictments of the Jerusalem leadership. Even in the rhetorical setting in which Luke is writing, some decades later, we are still very far from a definitive split between Judaism and Christianity. This is part of a sectarian controversy, a ding-dong argument between rival Jewish interpretations of the Bible that will rumble over the next few centuries. We cannot transfer Stephen's bitter denunciation of a particular group in his own context to a post-'parting' perspective, as if what Stephen says here is meant to be true of all Jews everywhere. Luke never says this (as we shall see), and in a post-Holocaust world it is not a stance that Christians can accept.

PRAYER

Father, we ask your forgiveness for the bigotry and prejudice that have soured relations between Jews and Christians over the centuries. Help us to work together for the restoration of your kingdom.

The FIRST CHRISTIAN MARTYR

I write these words on the anniversary of the terrorist attacks on the World Trade Center in New York in September 2001, an event etched on the minds of millions around the world who watched in horror as it unfolded on our TV screens. For many people, those events have problematized the very concept of martyrdom. Post-9/11, many would see 'martyrs' simply as religious fanatics with a reckless disregard for life, both their own and other people's. But it would be wrong to let this parody of martyrdom tarnish the biblical paradigm of martyrs as witnesses to their faith, prepared to stake their own lives—not the lives of others—on the truth they believe in. Stephen remains a challenge and an example for Christian witness in a world where many Christians are called to stake everything on their faith.

Paul's words in Acts 22:20 suggest that Stephen was already seen as the first Christian 'martyr', in the sense of someone who is prepared to die for his or her faith. But the word *martus* in Greek means first and foremost a witness—not an exhibitionist, not a spiritual athlete drawing attention to their own endurance capacities, but a witness pointing to a truth beyond themselves—and that is part of every Christian's calling. 'You will be my witnesses,' said Jesus to the Twelve (1:8), and later, to Saul, 'a witness to what you have seen and what you will see of me' (26:16). In other words, what we are here for is to provide living testimony to the transformative presence of God in his world. The witnesses at Stephen's lynching 'laid their coats at the feet of a young man named Saul' (v. 58), who thereby became implicated in the deed (as Paul himself implies at 22:20). But who can calculate what effect the manner of Stephen's death had on that young man?

Eyes fixed on the Lord

Alone in front of a hostile crowd, it would have been very easy to see nothing but hostile faces and gestures, but Stephen looks steadfastly upward (v. 55) and sees the glory beyond the pain. He sees the human figure of the crucified and rejected one standing in the place of ultimate honour and acceptance (v. 56). In the hour of extreme need, the martyr is sustained with a vision that sees further into reality than anyone else in the story has done so far. Where the apostles on the mountain saw only the cloud (1:9), Stephen sees right into the heart of heaven, to the centre of the universe. Without that vision there is no witness, only defiance: it is a risen and victorious Lord whom we serve.

This enables Stephen to put a proper value on his life. He was young (at least, we always assume so), vigorous, full of the Spirit (6:5), passionately engaged in life. He had a job to do (6:8), and the ability and spiritual gifts to do it. A martyr is not a person who is tired of life or has nothing better to do; but when that life is put at the service of another, it can be laid aside. It ceases to take centre stage. Preserving 'my' life, 'my' calling, 'my' work, is not the prime object any more.

Caught in the crossfire, following Jesus

Being a martyr takes courage: it is all too easy to duck out of conflict situations. There are times in all our lives when we have to stand up and be counted, when our witness to Christ has to face up to peer-group pressure, to society's expectations, to what's going on around us. Knowing when and how to do it is tricky, though. Christian witness isn't about courting trouble for its own sake, or about 'making a martyr of ourselves' in a kind of virtuous self-righteousness that won't win anyone to Christ.

Stephen's death, like his life, is modelled on that of his Lord. Just as Jesus committed his spirit to the Father (Luke 23:46), so Stephen entrusts his spirit to the Lord Jesus whom he has seen standing at God's right hand (v. 59). Even more strikingly, Stephen's last words are words of forgiveness for his persecutors (v. 60)—words paralleled by Jesus' own prayer from the cross (Luke 23:34). This is the final, costly realization of the principles that activated Jesus' life: 'Love your enemies… pray for those who abuse you' (Luke 6:27–28). Stephen's speech is polemical, passionate and at times harsh: here we see into his heart.

PRAYER

Grant, O Lord, that in all our sufferings here upon earth, for the testimony of thy truth, we may stedfastly behold the glory that shall be revealed; and, being filled with the Holy Ghost, may learn to love and bless our persecutors, by the example of thy first Martyr Stephen, who prayed for his murderers to thee, O blessed Jesus, who standest at the right hand of God to succour all those that suffer for thee, our only Mediator and Advocate. Amen.

Collect for St Stephen's day, Book of Common Prayer

24 ACTS 8:1–4

ACT TWO: JUDEA & SAMARIA

In Luke's four-act drama, Stephen's death marks the beginning of 'Act Two', the point where the gospel begins to move out from its first phase in Jerusalem and slowly, tentatively, becomes a worldwide mission. This is phase 2 of the original mission charge in 1:8, and it forms an essential bridge to the planned missionary journeys of phase 3 (chs. 13—28). Witness in 'Judea and Samaria' (8:1–25; 9:31) opens up surprising and unexpected horizons, as far afield as Ethiopia (8:26–39), down to the coastal towns of the Mediterranean (8:40; 9:32—10:48), and up to Syria and Cyprus (11:19). Slowly, painfully, the apostles and the Jerusalem church begin to face up to the questions, 'Exactly who is God speaking to? Who is the gospel for?' This initial expansion is anything but planned. In fact, what we see here is God's Spirit gradually moving the original witnesses out of their comfort zone, nudging them to raise their sights and broaden their horizons.

Introducing Saul

The new phase begins with an event that appears to be nothing short of a disaster. Verse 2 adds the final touch to the story of Stephen: despite his execution for blasphemy, pious men gave him proper burial—perhaps a hint that not everyone in the Jewish community agreed with the council's decision. Verse 1, on the other hand, introduces a new storyline, carrying the gospel out far beyond the confines of the city—and a new hero, who is going to dominate the story from chapter 13 onwards. Up to this point, Saul is merely a hidden presence, lurking ominously in the background of Stephen's story as a witness to Stephen's death (7:58). Now Luke brings him a little more into the foreground, telling us that he was fully in agreement with the execution. He is not taking part, apparently—just holding the coats—but something about that event propelled Saul to become active in persecution, ravaging the church in a classic portrayal of intolerant and out-of-control religious fanaticism.

Luke's picture is close enough to Paul's own description of this phase of his life to make sense (see Galatians 1; Philippians 3; 1 Corinthians 15). The detail that he was a young man (7:58), coupled

68

with Paul's own half-shamefaced, half-boasting admission that he had outclassed his contemporaries in zeal (Galatians 1:14), adds up to a familiar type on the contemporary religious scene. Saul was a radical young fundamentalist, top of his class and busting to change the world to his own way of thinking, irrespective of the cost to himself or to anyone else.

Exile—or mission field?

Perhaps one of the things that spurred Saul on to get actively involved in the mission to wipe out the new sect was its surprising success: verse 3 provides the first confirmation in Acts that this rapidly expanding movement included women as well as men. But Jerusalem is no longer a safe haven for the believers. Stephen's confrontation with the Sanhedrin seems to have stirred up so much anger and bitterness that it sparked off a concentrated attempt to root out the whole of this troublesome sect—although the fact that the apostles were able to remain in Jerusalem (v. 1) may suggest that it was particularly the 'Hellenists' who were affected.

Being scattered (vv. 1, 4) is not necessarily a bad thing, however. At least some of those who are expelled from Jerusalem see it as an opportunity rather than a threat, and start preaching the word as they go about through the countryside of Judea and Samaria. So the church begins to fulfil the mission charge laid upon the original disciples in 1:8, although, humanly speaking, it happens more or less by accident. Also (as so often in Acts), what Luke doesn't tell us is as interesting as what he does. Who was responsible for this momentous development? Clearly not the apostles, who were left behind in Jerusalem (v. 1). The inference is that it must have been ordinary believers, acting under the Spirit's guidance and without any express instructions from the leadership of the church. So often, we find that the only way the church begins to grow is when we allow ourselves to be forced out of our comfort zone and begin to trust the Spirit.

REFLECTION

Declare God's praise before the nations, you who are the children of Israel: For if our God has scattered you amongst them, there too has he shown you his greatness.

Tobit 13:3–4 (RSV)

25

ACTS 8:5–13

MISSION *in* SAMARIA

Like Stephen, Philip has a Greek name, so was probably one of the 'Hellenists' from the Greek-speaking Jewish community in Jerusalem (6:5). Like Stephen, too, he was originally commissioned to serve at table (6:2–3), but finds himself entrusted with a wider vocation.

Our friends in the north

Restoration is the first of the two major underlying themes in Luke's account of Philip's mission in Samaria. In the geographical schema of 1:8, Samaria holds a special place. It is not just an intermediate stage, one step further out from Jerusalem; it is also part of greater Israel, the old northern kingdom. Philip's mission symbolically reunites the old northern and southern kingdoms of Israel and Judah in the new kingdom era ushered in by God's anointed Messiah (compare 1:6). So there is a very definite eschatological (end-time) dimension to Luke's geography here, with undertones of the restoration and reconciliation of long-sundered branches of God's people.

Exactly where Philip's mission takes place is not clear. Some manuscripts read 'the city of Samaria' in verse 5, recalling the ancient capital of the northern kingdom, but in Philip's time Samaria was an ethnic region, not a city. Luke is more concerned to portray a mission to the Samaritan people, who lived not in the rebuilt Greek city of Sebaste but in scattered villages across the uplands, so it probably makes sense to go with the alternative reading, 'a city of [the region of] Samaria' (as in John 4:5). Either way, Luke uses geographical names in a way that brings out the theological significance of the events he describes.

Magic and miracle

This is also a story about power—different kinds of spiritual power, and its use and abuse. Philip's one object was to preach Christ to the Samaritans (v. 5), and he found in so doing that the signs and wonders that had accompanied Jesus' mission in Galilee and Judea were now spilling over into Samaria. People paid attention to what Philip said (v. 6) because they could see as well as hear the effective presence of God's energetic Spirit in his words (v. 7). Just as in the

Gospel, the effect of an encounter with the living Christ is an out-pouring of wholeness and joy (v. 8).

Christians, though, are not the only ones who can exercise spiritual power in Luke's story, and the Samaritans already had their own miracle worker. Simon (v. 9) had already established a nice line in wonder-working, and had the reputation of embodying 'the power of God that is called Great' in his community (v. 10). Amazement, not joy, is the result of his activity, which Luke labels 'magic'—a label that identifies Simon not as a charlatan but as a rival. Later Christian tradition knows Simon Magus as the first heretic, founder of a Samaritan cult that is seen as a forerunner of Gnosticism and comes to a dramatic confrontation with Peter in Rome.

The real thing

On the surface, the contest between Philip and Simon looks like a competition between two rival manifestations of spiritual power—a contest between magicians, we might say, rather like the contest between Elijah and the prophets of Baal in 1 Kings 18. On the face of it, it's not obvious how we are to choose between them: is it the one that shouts loudest, or the one who performs the most impressive wonders? This is a problem that preoccupies Luke, and he will return to it in chapters 13, 19 and 28. So part of what Luke is doing here is to set up the first of a series of confrontations which explore the nature of spiritual power and the boundaries between magic and miracle.

The simple fact is that there is no contest. Simon, as well as his audi-ence, instinctively realizes that what Philip is offering is the real thing, not just bigger and better miracles but something qualitatively different that demands a real commitment to spiritual transformation. Philip's message is about the kingdom of God and the name of Jesus Christ (v. 12). One cannot be attained without the other, and there is much more involved than the immediate gratification of sensationalism. That's why baptism is the logical response (v. 13): it means a funda-mental change of heart ('repentance', 2:38), and a personal commit-ment to becoming part of God's kingdom-plans through faith in the person of Christ ('in the name of the Lord Jesus', 8:16).

PRAYER

Father, help us to recognize that true spiritual power comes from following in the footsteps of the one who laid down his life for others.

26

MAGIC & MONEY

Now the Twelve in Jerusalem hear rumours that Samaria has accepted the word of God, preached in the name of Jesus. Given the history of bad blood between Samaria and Jerusalem (see Luke 9:51–56; John 4), it is perhaps not surprising that they send Peter and John to investigate.

The apostles and the evangelist

Luke, like Paul, takes a strategic view of the economy of mission: a successful mission in one Samaritan town means that 'Samaria has received the word of God' (v. 14). This is not so much exaggeration as *pars pro toto*, a manner of thinking that sees the whole as implied in the part (compare 19:10, or Paul in Romans 15). It implies that the job of the evangelist is to plant the seeds in a region and let God do the rest. But there is one more thing needed before Philip can move on. Philip has baptized his converts in the name of the Lord Jesus, but they have not yet received the Holy Spirit (v. 16). They have been incorporated into a larger whole, but (like many Christians today) they do not yet realize the full implications of what has happened to them. The full process of Christian baptism in water and Spirit (Mark 1:8) involves both a turning away from the old life and a turning towards the new, both saying 'No' to the sins and failures of the past (*metanoia*, repentance) and saying 'Yes' to the new life that God has on offer. The gift of the Holy Spirit is what gives Christians the power to stand on their own two feet and grow in the spiritual life. It is an essential part of all Christians' experience (compare 2:38–39), not just of those called to a particular ministry (6:3–5).

The gift of the Spirit

Instead of calling down the fire of judgment, then, the apostles find themselves calling down the fiery presence of God's Holy Spirit on the Samaritans (v. 15). Here Luke makes the baptism and reception of the Spirit a two-stage process, with the apostles coming down from Jerusalem to 'confirm' the new believers by the laying on of hands (v. 17). This is the biblical model for the practice of 'confirmation' by a bishop in many churches (a similar pattern can be seen at 19:1–7).

Churches in the Pentecostal/charismatic tradition work with a rather different two-stage model, seeing 'baptism in the Spirit' as a distinct experience. But, as we shall see, Luke does not always present a consistent pattern in Acts (compare 8:36–38, where the Spirit is not mentioned, or 10:44–48, where the Spirit comes first). What is important is not the order or the manner in which they are experienced, but that both are essential to the Christian life.

The apostles and the magician

As we have seen, Luke is careful all along to distinguish the miraculous power of the Spirit from magic. This story progressively unfolds some of the essential differences. Simon claims a name for himself (8:9), while Philip and the apostles do everything in the name of Jesus (8:5, 12, 16). Simon basks in the admiration of his community, using his powers to advance his own status (8:9–10); Philip fades quietly into the background when the apostles arrive (vv. 14–25) and moves on when his work is done (8:26), trusting his converts to their Lord. Simon seeks to attach people to himself; Philip and the apostles aim to integrate them into a community. Simon sees spiritual power as a force to be manipulated and controlled (vv. 18–19); the apostles see it as a gift from God (v. 20).

Money in Acts frequently functions as a touchstone for distinguishing true from false in the realm of the Spirit (compare 3:6; 5:3). What God gives is pure gift: it transcends our value-system, so it cannot become part of a commercial transaction. Peter's rebuke to Simon underlines how important it is for this fledgling community to put a proper value on a gift which is literally 'priceless' (vv. 20–23). You cannot calculate the financial value of ministry. Being allowed to participate in God's dealings with his people is both above and below the profit/loss accounts of human financial systems.

PRAYER

Remember, O Lord, what you have wrought in us, and not what we deserve; and as you have called us to your service, so make us worthy of our calling: through Jesus Christ our Lord.

Leonine Sacramentary

SHOW ME *the* WAY

What has Philip been doing all this while? Luke does not tell us, but Philip's role is becoming more clearly defined as that of an evangelist (see 21:8) rather than a church-builder. The apostles themselves briefly become itinerant missionaries on their way home (v. 25), but for Philip, itinerancy is the essence of what he does. He is attuned to God's guidance (v. 26), ready to take off at the drop of a hat and journey into the emptiness of a desert landscape, to await whatever encounter God has in store.

Hitting the road

This is a story of intersecting journeys. Philip's route-map is precise: head due south to intercept the Jerusalem–Gaza highway, and then wait and see. What he sees, just as he arrives at this desolate spot, is a chariot bowling along the road. It bears perhaps the last person he would have expected to see—an African pilgrim from the ancient and romantic kingdom of Ethiopia. 'Eunuch' (v. 27) could be a physical description, or it could simply describe an official function at the court. ('Candace', incidentally, is a royal title, not the name of an Ethiopian queen.) So the eunuch is a court official, used to authority and luxury. He is also a pilgrim: he has been up to Jerusalem to pray in the temple. On the mental map of the ancient Mediterranean world, Ethiopia is part of the 'ends of the earth' (1:8). But in religious terms, the Ethiopian is a figure of the borderlands, halfway between Jew and Gentile, either a God-fearer or (more likely) a full convert to Judaism.

Reading and understanding

The eunuch is not only wealthy but also learned, learned enough to be able to read Isaiah (apparently) in Hebrew (v. 28). God has been preparing the way for this most improbable of encounters, but Philip doesn't know this until he gets close enough (v. 29) to hear what the distinguished foreigner is reading aloud to himself. Philip's question (v. 30) perhaps reflects some surprise that this non-Jewish pilgrim should be able to read the Hebrew text with understanding. For a high court official, literacy was a necessity. Nevertheless, many (if not most) Jews in first-century Palestine needed the help of an Aramaic paraphrase to understand the Hebrew text.

Preaching the good news

Underlying this apparently mundane conversation is a fundamental principle of Lucan exegesis. Quite apart from language problems, scripture is not self-interpreting: Spirit-inspired guidance is required to unpack the true significance of the Hebrew scriptures. The Isaiah scroll is open at one of the key texts of early Christian apologetic, part of the great 'Servant Songs' of Isaiah 53, which portray God's 'servant' as a despised, wounded, rejected figure, the very antithesis of the victorious Messiah of Jewish expectation (vv. 32–33). But who is this mysterious 'servant'? The Ethiopian's question (v. 34) is a reasonable one, which continues to puzzle students of the Hebrew Bible, but for Philip the evangelist there can be only one answer. The Isaiah passage holds a vital clue to the paradox of a suffering Saviour, wounded for his people's transgressions and suffering before entering into his glory. This is not the anticipated Messiah of popular expectation, but nevertheless a figure firmly rooted in scripture. So the Hebrew text, properly interpreted, becomes a vehicle for preaching the good news (v. 35), a Way that leads straight to baptism (vv. 36–38).

On the Way

And then? We can speculate about what happened next (in Ethiopian tradition, the eunuch went home and founded the Ethiopic church). In Luke's story, though, what is important is the roadside encounter itself, a point of intersection with no before and after—or rather, where the before and after are known only to God. Philip is caught up by the Spirit (vv. 39–40) and disappears from the story at this point until chapter 21; and all we know (and need to know) of the Ethiopian is that this is the beginning of a new journey, a journey suffused with joy (v. 39).

FOR DISCUSSION AND PRAYER

'You know my journeys and my resting-places, and are acquainted with all my ways' (Psalm 139:2). Pray for the people you will encounter on your journey today.

28

ACTS 9:1–9

The ROAD *to* DAMASCUS

This is a story that meant a lot to Paul. He refers to it several times in his letters, and Luke has him retell it twice when he is on trial for his life (Acts 22; 26). This is the memory he turns to when he has to explain, 'Who am I? How did I get here?' The key moment in his life was his meeting with Jesus on the Damascus road, a meeting of enormous significance not only for Paul but for the whole history of the church. But we can also read this story from the personal angle, as a story of God's call and how it changes real human lives.

A change of direction

We call this event Paul's 'conversion', but actually the word is rather misleading. We generally use it to describe a change from unbelief to belief, or a change from one religion to another, but Paul already believed in God, and it is much too early at this stage to think of Judaism and Christianity as two separate 'religions'. Paul himself describes the event as an encounter with the risen Jesus, the last of the resurrection appearances (1 Corinthians 15:8–10). He also uses the language of 'vision' (1 Corinthians 15:8; Acts 26:19) and of a prophetic 'calling' (Galatians 1:15, echoing Jeremiah 1:5). But Luke's very concrete account highlights that it was, above all, a dramatic change of direction. Saul was the top student of his year, full of zeal, busily engaged in serving God—but going the wrong way (v. 1). He was on a journey, going after a bunch of idiots who called themselves 'the Way' (v. 2), a way that Saul had no intention of following. His idea was to turn them round, by force if need be, and bring them back into the fold. Unfortunately for Saul's plans, the opposite happened. The 'Way' that looked all wrong turned out to be the right way, and it was Saul who had to change direction.

Called by name

There is a voice, calling Saul by name (v. 4). All Luke's three accounts of this event stress the double naming: 'Saul, Saul'. This was Paul's Hebrew name, the name that established his family tree and national identity (Philippians 3:5), the name (doubtless) in which he took all his academic awards at the university in Jerusalem (Galatians 1:14).

God's call is always directed to the real person. It's easy to say, 'No, Lord, you've got the wrong person', but God's call says, 'No, it's you I want, you with all that history and genetic make-up, all the things you're proud of as well as the things you wish hadn't happened—all that goes to make up the real you.'

A reversal of perceptions

There is also a heavenly light (v. 3): the call comes in such a way that Saul cannot doubt that it is from God. Saul, who is trying so hard to serve God, can only say, 'Lord, I don't know who you are'; and the answer comes, 'I am Jesus, the one you are persecuting' (v. 5). Saul was convinced that Jesus was the wrong Way, the one who was leading all these other poor souls astray, and now he speaks with God's authority, is standing (as Stephen had claimed in 7:56) at the right hand of God. This was precisely what Gamaliel had warned his fellow councillors of (5:39), and it is a terrifying discovery.

Learning dependence

There is a tradition in paintings of this story that Saul was riding a horse on his way to Damascus. There is no horse in Luke's story, but the dramatic fall is there (v. 4): the arrogant persecutor who knows what's right for everyone else becomes humiliated (literally 'on the ground'). Moreover, he is blinded, has to be led by the hand (v. 8), and will spend three days in the dark (v. 9), waiting to be told what to do (v. 6). There could hardly be a better way to dramatize the complete revaluation that Saul experienced. Before he could work for God, he would have to learn dependence on God's grace. Paul himself puts it this way in Philippians 3:7: 'Whatever gain I had, I counted as loss for the sake of Christ.'

PRAYER

Lord, we find it so hard to hear your call. Help us to accept our complete dependence on your grace.

The HAND of FELLOWSHIP

There's a story of the newly appointed minister who stood up to preach in his new church and announced, 'My job is to find out what God is doing here—and get in on the act.' Acts is all about finding out what God is doing out there in the world. But it can be disconcerting to discover when and how God is at work: God's horizons are always so much wider than ours.

A disciple called Ananias

Ananias only has a walk-on part, yet he plays a pivotal role in the drama of Acts. He was the person whom God chose to release Saul from his imprisoned and blinded state into full and active faith. He is not an apostle, simply a disciple, one of the many unsung heroes and heroines of Luke's story. But the essence is that, like Samuel and Isaiah (1 Samuel 3:10; Isaiah 6:1–8), he was ready to say, 'Here I am, Lord' when God spoke to him. Like Philip, he receives precise directions (v. 11), but unlike Philip, he is told whom he is going to meet: a man called Saul, who is praying. That's all he needs to know, all that matters to God. Time and time again in Acts, when believers muster up the courage to speak of their faith, they discover that God has got there first. When we left Saul, he was being led, sightless and fumbling, into a safe house somewhere in Damascus (9:8). Now we discover that he wasn't doing nothing during his three-day fast: waiting in the darkness, he was learning to listen, waiting on God.

You cannot be serious!

It may be enough for God—but it isn't enough for Ananias! He knows a lot about Saul, none of it reassuring. He knows exactly why Saul has come to Damascus (vv. 13–14). So we have the slightly comic picture (but haven't we all done it?) of Ananias arguing with God, trying to tell God his business: 'Lord, you don't know this guy!' But God does know Saul—knows the very worst about him—and still chooses him. It's a paradox that Paul, when he looks back on his life years later, sees only too well: election and grace go hand in hand (see 1 Corinthians 15; Philippians 3; 1 Timothy 1:12–16).

To reveal his Son in me

Precisely what God has in mind for Saul's future becomes clearer in subsequent retellings of this story (see chs. 22; 26). Looking back, we can see that the seeds of the future mission to the Gentiles are here already, but it will take Saul/Paul quite some time to work out exactly what his vocation means. For the moment, all he needs to know is that it's a call to testify, and a call to suffer (v. 16).

The privilege of vocation cannot be divorced from the privilege of suffering. If God chooses to 'reveal his Son in me' (Galatians 1:16), it's my whole life that's on the line, not just my words. There is a robustness about this view of vocation which at least has the merit of being realistic. Nobody ever said that the Christian life would be easy, and perhaps it's just as well that we don't know quite what lies around the corner. But there is reassurance here too: the way may be hard, but Christ will be a part of it.

Brother Saul

Ananias' capitulation, once he gets the point, is unreserved. There's no grudging welcome for the black sheep, no 'I'll be keeping an eye on you'. Nor does he attempt to ration out the privileges of being a believer ('Wait till you've been here a few years'). For Ananias, whatever the convert's past, once he's accepted, he's in—welcomed as a brother, sharing all the blessings of physical healing and spiritual reorientation.

Formally speaking, the laying on of hands here (v. 17) is not apostolic. Ananias was not one of the Twelve, and there is no record that he himself was ever commissioned by the Jerusalem apostles. He acts simply as a believer, responding directly to the vision out of the conviction that he too has been sent (v. 17) by the same Lord Jesus who appeared to Saul on the road. For Luke (as for Paul: see Galatians 1:12), Paul's apostolic commission came not from Jerusalem but direct from the Lord himself. So Saul's Damascus road experience leads him into a transformative encounter with the risen Christ. Its results are vision restored, rising to new life, baptism and filling with the Holy Spirit (vv. 17–18), and renewed strength (v. 19).

PRAYER

Say a prayer of thanksgiving for all the anonymous, 'unimportant' people who helped you along the road to faith.

30 ACTS 9:20–30

A CONVERT *in* TROUBLE

No half measures for Saul! The apostle Paul (as he was to become) later described his early years as full of 'zeal': a consuming ambition to do better than any of his classmates in seminary, a passionate commitment to putting the world right for God and eradicating those who were getting God wrong, a burning zeal for the interpretative tradition that showed how God's revelation was to be read in the world (Galatians 1:13–14). As he later testified of his fellow Jews, he bore 'a zeal for God—only it was not enlightened' (Romans 10:2).

Testifying to the Christ

That zeal is immediately turned, with all the enthusiasm of the convert, against his former allies and employers (v. 20). Saul now spends his time in synagogue arguing vociferously that Jesus is the Son of God and Christ (v. 22). Not surprisingly, this sudden volte-face meets with a stormy reception: amazement and wonder (v. 21), confusion but no conviction (v. 22). Saul's Damascus journey, which started with such grand ambitions, ends in an ignominious escape over the wall in a basket (vv. 23–25). This was probably not as precarious as it sounds: basketware slings are still used today in the Middle East for hoisting bricks and timber on building sites. Paul himself describes this episode in 2 Corinthians 11:32–33 in tones suggesting that he saw the whole thing in a distinctly anti-heroic light. He also gives a slightly different spin to the story: Luke focuses on the hostility of 'the Jews' (v. 23), while Paul attributes the problem to the ethnarch (NRSV 'governor') of the Nabatean King Aretas.

This incidentally gives us a chronological framework for the episode, which suggests that a longer period has elapsed than we might think from the account in Acts. (Luke is supremely uninterested in dates, and his 'after many days', v. 23, is not a great deal of help.) Aretas was ruler over the kingdom of Nabatea from 8BC to AD39/40, and seems to have been given some kind of political control over Damascus by the emperor Gaius Caligula after the death of Tiberius in AD37. The Nabateans drew a large part of their revenues from the caravan trade, and there was a colony of Nabatean merchants resident in Damascus.

The ugly duckling

The fact is, however, that Saul the convert is still in a very raw and unfledged state, marginalized not only by his old allies but also by his new 'brothers'. Although the disciples in Damascus (following Ananias' example) are prepared to accept him (v. 19), the community in Jerusalem is highly suspicious (v. 26). Anthropologists speak of a period of 'liminality', a 'wilderness experience' essential to the integration of any religious vision or vocation at a deep personal level. Maybe the disciples in Jerusalem thought that his zeal was doing more harm than good (vv. 29–30), but in fact Saul needed time alone with his God before he could begin to learn what it would mean for God to reveal his Son in his life (compare v. 16).

Enter Barnabas

The role of an advocate and protector is vital in this precarious state, and Barnabas is the crucial catalyst, the friend and 'godfather' who welcomes the new convert, introduces him to the apostles, tells his story (v. 27), and sends him away for a period out of the limelight (v. 30). In Galatians 1:17, Paul speaks of a period in Arabia before returning to Damascus, and stresses the brevity of his visit to Jerusalem in order to emphasize his independence of the apostles (Galatians 1:18–20). Both accounts agree that after visiting Jerusalem, Saul went home to Tarsus in the province of Cilicia (v. 30; Galatians 1:21), to wait quietly (maybe some years) before Barnabas came to find him and bring him back to play an active role in the life of the church in Antioch (11:25–26). But that is still in the future. Saul has met Christ, he's begun his journey, there are hints of great things to come, but for the moment he has to watch on the sidelines, waiting for the full significance of his vocation to unfold in God's good time.

FOR DISCUSSION AND PRAYER

How difficult is it for new converts to become integrated into the life of your church? Who plays the Barnabas role there?

BESIDE *the* SEASIDE

Luke's storyline in this middle section of the book looks rather randomly arranged, but in fact there's a clear progression, leading up to chapter 10, where Peter will meet the Gentile Cornelius. First, though, Peter has to be winkled out of Jerusalem so that he can be in the right place to discover what God is doing out in the rest of the world.

The church in Judea

Luke marks the bridge to a new scene with a summary verse (v. 31) which links back to 1:8, showing us that everything in this section is part of the witness in 'Judea and Samaria'. The dispersed believers have done their job well: working outwards from Jerusalem, the church is now well established in the whole of Judea and Galilee and Samaria. There are no hints here of continued persecution, or of the controversy that dogged Saul's visit to Jerusalem. This is a picture of peaceful consolidation as the church learns to 'walk in the fear of the Lord' (an Old Testament phrase expressing the ideal of an ordered society: see Psalm 19:9; Proverbs 1:7) and is filled with the comfort of the Holy Spirit (not just a one-off experience, but a characteristic of the ongoing life of the renewed people of God).

An itinerant ministry

This section shows how the apostolic role is changing in a rapidly expanding network of believers. First comes the realization that their own special charism within the people of God is the ministry of word and prayer (6:4); others can be trusted, under the guidance of the Spirit, to handle administrative and charitable work. In chapter 8 they discover that they do not have a monopoly on evangelization: here, too, others can be trusted to preach the word and baptize new believers. So the apostles begin to move into an oversight role, integrating new communities into the wider network and ensuring the continuity of their ongoing spiritual life with the Pentecost experience (8:14–17). This is the role that Peter continues here, moving about among them all (v. 32), visiting the tiny enclaves of God's people ('the saints') in Lydda and Joppa (vv. 32, 38), leaving his base in Jerusalem and moving into a more mobile role.

A healing ministry

In so doing, Peter rediscovers the essence of apostolic ministry in following, and imitating, his Master's lifestyle. Ministry 'on the road', ministry bringing real lives into a healing encounter with the power of God, is exactly how Jesus spent his time, and the healings of Aeneas and Tabitha show Peter following Jesus' example and taking the healing power of the kingdom out from Jerusalem and right down to the coastal plain. The difference is that Peter does nothing in his own name or by his own power. It is the healing power of Jesus Christ that brings wholeness and new life (v. 34), and brings another whole region to turn to the Lord (v. 35). Lydda (modern Lod) is on the very edge of the hill-country of Judea; the Sarona (Hebrew *Sharon*) refers to the wooded area on the coastal plain between Joppa (modern Jaffa) and Caesarea. It's a marginal region in every respect: coastland, facing out across the Mediterranean, much more open to the cosmopolitan influences of the Hellenistic and Roman world, and largely settled by Greeks.

Down to the coast

God's next move brings Peter himself right down to the coast. Joppa was not in his travel plans: the impulse comes from the disciples in Joppa, distraught at a death within the community. Amazed to hear that Peter is as close as Lydda, they send a small deputation to beg him to come (v. 38). 'Do not hesitate' is a polite form of request, but it suggests that Peter might have had reason to hesitate before going as far as the coast. For a Galilean fisherman, this was unknown territory. Tabitha's name (v. 36) means 'gazelle' (Luke gives the name both in Hebrew and Greek), and she was obviously a gentle and much-loved member of the community, expressing her discipleship (Luke uses the feminine form *mathetria*) forcefully and effectively by using the traditional women's skills of weaving and making garments to benefit the needy (vv. 36–37, 39). Once again, Peter brings the healing power of his Master into a hopeless situation and finds life renewed and faith reinvigorated (vv. 40–42).

PRAYER

Pray for all whose ministry leads them into an oversight role: for strength and sustenance on the road, and that they may never lose sight of the Master whose lifestyle they seek to follow.

SEASIDE LODGING

All this apparently random wandering—responding to a call here, taking a few days' rest there—brings Peter to the right place at the right time for one of the most momentous scenes in the book, a scene so important that it gets told three times over, once by Luke as it happens (ch. 10), and twice by Peter as he reflects on it (chs. 11; 15).

At the house of the tanner

Small narrative details underline the precariousness of Peter's position. He is lodging, staying as a guest, accepting hospitality, with Simon the tanner in his house beside the sea in Joppa (9:43; 10:6). Hospitality is going to be a major theme of this episode: watch out for who offers it, who accepts it, and what are the difficulties and implications of accepting it.

The Greek word *xenos* means both 'guest' and 'stranger', and there is a hint that Peter is very much a stranger in town. He is already taking a risk by staying with a tanner. The craft of the tanner was a necessary one in the ancient world, but the smelliness of its processes meant that tanneries tended to be sited on the edge of town, preferably downwind (you can see this in the Roman city of Barcina, beneath modern-day Barcelona). So it is natural that the tanner's house would be beside the sea, but the detail is significant for a story that wastes very little time on incidental detail and for an author who chooses his words as carefully as Luke does. In Luke's Gospel, the 'sea of Galilee', where Peter grew up and worked as a fisherman, is called a lake (*limne*). For Luke, the real sea (*thalassa*) is the Mediterranean, a lurking menace on the edge of Hebrew nightmare, a place of storm and sea-monster, opening up horizons to the wider world. Peter doesn't get to travel on the sea in Luke's story—only Paul does—but here is Peter, beside the seaside, about to have his horizons dramatically enlarged.

Cornelius the centurion

First, we have to meet a new character, important enough to have a personal introduction and a whole scene to himself. Cornelius lives in Caesarea (10:1), a coastal city that embodies all the ambiguities of

Jewish identity. It is the seat of Roman government for the province of Judea, a port and trade centre, but also a thriving Greek city where Herod located the baths and hippodrome that he didn't dare build in more conservative Jerusalem. The name Cornelius is a good patrician Roman name which he (or his family) probably got from a patron, and he is a centurion in the Italian cohort. Suddenly we're in another world, the brusque military world of the Roman empire, a reminder of the huge and complex imperial framework that encloses Peter and his small community. As a centurion, Cornelius wouldn't be top-brass himself—centurions were the senior warrant officers of the Roman army—but he would be a considerable swell in the eyes of the natives.

A man who fears God

Yet Cornelius is also a pious and God-fearing man, one who (like the centurion of Luke 7:1–9) is respected by the local Jewish community and finds himself drawn to the high spiritual and charitable ideals of the synagogue. This is the first mention in Acts of a group that is going to play an important role in the story. The 'God-fearers' were righteous Gentiles who attended synagogue worship and supported the Jewish community in vital ways, both financial and political (see comment on 13:16). Luke depicts him as fulfilling all the demands of Jewish piety (v. 2) except one: he is a Gentile.

A soldier's vision

As so often in Acts, the key moment in this story is a moment of vision (10:3), a vision that is repeated three times as the story unfolds (10:22, 30–32; 11:13). Cornelius is faithful in observing the regular hours of prayer (10:30). It's a moment when God takes the initiative, speaking to the outsider by name (long before Peter is even aware that such a person exists), and giving him precise instructions which Cornelius has no hesitation in taking seriously.

PRAYER

God of surprises, thank you that your horizons are always
so much wider than ours.

33

PETER'S CHALLENGE

By running two narrative threads at once, Luke makes it abundantly clear that the action in this story is happening on two fronts simultaneously: God is at work both inside and outside the church. This is going to be a crucial point in the argument later on, when Peter and James have to justify this encounter to the church at large. It was God who took the first step (15:7, 14).

Lunch break

Cornelius' messengers have started on their fateful journey (v. 9); the next step is to ensure that Peter is prepared to make them welcome. Peter, of course, has no clue what is about to happen. He just goes up to the roof of the tanner's house about midday to say his prayers. Having regular times for prayer is something that Luke takes for granted as a normal feature of the apostles' lives. Maybe Peter also wanted a breath of fresh sea air above the reek of the tanning-vats. He was not deliberately fasting, but he was extremely hungry (v. 10), perhaps listening with half an ear for the sounds of dinner being prepared down below. (Praying doesn't prevent our normal human responses to hunger!)

In this state of heightened anticipation, Peter falls into a trance (Greek *ekstasis*, literally 'standing outside oneself') and has a vision (v. 11). It's a vision of food, but a bizarre and disgusting one. He sees the heavens opened—a remarkable event in itself, one that normally portends a moment of significant revelation (see Luke 3:21; Acts 7:56). But what comes down is almost bathetic. It's a huge sheet held up over the earth by its four corners, and bulging with a motley collection of animals, reptiles and flying creatures (v. 12). Then Peter hears a heavenly voice (v. 13), which says, 'You're hungry—so get up and help yourself.'

Unknown waters

'No way,' says Peter. 'I have never yet eaten anything common or unclean' (v. 14). The words highlight his sense of standing on the brink of unknown waters: I'm safe, I know my values, I've always worked within fixed boundaries. And, rhetorically speaking, this is the answer that an orthodox Jewish community would respect and approve. Up to now, nothing in Acts—at least in Peter's experience—has transgressed the purity laws. This makes the response of the heavenly voice all the more shocking: what God has cleansed, *you* (emphatic pronoun in the Greek) must not 'soil' (v. 15). The word is hard to translate. It can mean either to 'make something unclean' or to 'call something unclean'. So is it about labels, or about reality? The answer is both, because, in a purity context, labels create reality. The next question is: whose labels? Who actually has the right to label some parts of God's creation 'pure', fit for human consumption, and others not? Who gets to decide?

Making distinctions

The vision happens three times (v. 16), and each time the vessel with its bizarre, indiscriminate cargo is taken up into heaven—the same words that Luke had used of Jesus' bodily ascension (1:2, 11). And, like the ascension (how can a human body ascend to heaven?), it leaves us—with Peter—wondering (v. 17) if heaven is a stranger (and perhaps more interesting) place than we had thought. What are all these creatures doing up there? Is heaven perhaps less discriminating than we are?

This, it turns out, is precisely the question Peter has to wrestle with. It's not really about food (although food will come into it), but it is about discrimination, making hard and fast distinctions between people and labelling some as OK, insiders, and some as outsiders, unclean. Now the real test of Peter's discrimination is standing below, knocking at the door (vv. 18–19), even as he rubs his eyes and scratches his head and wonders what the vision was all about (v. 19). 'Go down,' says the Spirit, 'and go with them without making distinctions [v. 20], because I [emphatic pronoun] have sent them.'

Whose problem?

What is at the heart of Peter's problem? Most readers of this commentary are probably (like me) Gentile Christians, so it's easy to label Peter's problem as a Jewish thing, something to do with 'the Jewish Law' or Jewish dietary regulations. But labels create artificial lines here, lines between 'them' and 'us'. To understand how it looks from Peter's viewpoint, we have to ask, 'Who told him that certain foods were unclean?' The answer is, the Bible—God's revelatory word (see Leviticus 11).

FOR DISCUSSION AND PRAYER

'It's not difference that creates the problem, but discrimination.'

Desmond Tutu

34 ACTS 10:21–29

STRANGERS & GUESTS

One of the remarkable things about this story is the way Luke slows down the narrative pace by giving us all sorts of unnecessary detail about travel and hospitality that he doesn't normally bother with. It has the effect of filming in slow motion—another way to highlight how important this episode is for the whole story of Acts. It's Luke's way of saying, 'This is a God moment: something is happening here, so pay attention.' It's worth taking time to read the whole thing in slow motion, not skipping over the detail but savouring it and using it to get inside the characters' skins. For a group, that could mean doing a dramatic reading, using different characters in different parts of the room.

A knock at the door

From this point on, Peter is in unknown waters, trying to be attentive to what God is revealing in the situation as it unfolds. The first step is to go down (v. 21), down from the place of vision into the confusion of everyday life, down to meet the three men knocking at the door and accept the God-given role that they are pushing him into: 'Yes, it's me you're looking for.' Who knows what that action cost Peter? But everything else flows from that initial acceptance. Then he can begin to ask questions, to listen, to hear the other side of the story.

His question allows the visitors to tell their own story—which we know, but Peter doesn't—in their own words, adding some significant details (v. 22): Cornelius is a righteous man, vouchsafed for by the Jewish community. All of this only serves to underline the inescapable fact that he is a Gentile, not 'one of us'. Nevertheless, he has been visited by an angel, a divine messenger, who sent the human messengers on their mysterious errand. So what have they come for? In a sense, they don't know either. They've come for a word that nobody in the story can yet envisage, a word that Peter himself doesn't yet know.

Come on in

Hospitality is the next step (v. 23). The strangers have to be welcomed in—but at first on Peter's own terms. From Peter's point of view, it's not too difficult to invite Gentile visitors in to share table-fellowship in a Jewish home, to share what he has and become part of his way of life. The next step is bolder: to go out with them and allow his strange guests to lead him somewhere new, to become a guest (and therefore a stranger) himself. It is a sensible precaution for Peter to take some of the brothers with him, as an escort, as a guarantee of safety, as witnesses (compare 11:12). But it is also an added risk. It means trusting the strangers enough (or trusting God enough) to risk taking others with him on a journey into the unknown.

Crossing the threshold

The sense of heightened anticipation on Peter's arrival in Caesarea is palpable (v. 24). Cornelius is expecting him: he has even got a houseful of friends and relatives there as a reception committee (a leap of faith if ever there was one!). What were they thinking? Did they wonder if their friend had taken leave of his senses? Who were they waiting for? Hence the extravagant gestures when (against all odds) Peter finally appears on cue (v. 25). Cornelius tries to kneel to Peter, to treat him as a messenger of the gods—only to be gently rebuffed. So the meeting starts (as all such meetings must) with the fundamental recognition that both parties are human beings, a recognition that creates a crucial platform for what follows. 'I'm here in God's name,' Peter says, 'but that doesn't put me on a different plane from you. I'm here because God is calling me—but so are you.' In that confidence, he can take the momentous step of crossing the threshold (vv. 27–28).

Receiving hospitality, becoming a guest, is often much more difficult than giving it. We are not on our own turf; we have to learn to live by somebody else's rules. There's no neutral territory here, no 'safe house' where we can get to know one another. Either you are my guest, or I'm yours: either you learn to live by my rules, or I learn to live by yours. Or is there another way? That's essentially what Peter is on a quest to discover.

FOR DISCUSSION AND PRAYER

Peter's story is a challenge to come down from our isolated rooftops and come out from behind the barricades we build up between ourselves and the 'other'. How far are we prepared to travel to meet the strangers outside our churches on their own ground?

35

ACTS 10:30–48

A SERMON & ITS AFTERMATH

It's a strange feeling to be the answer to someone else's prayers! The multiple retellings of this story allow Luke to highlight the impact of Peter's vision on three different groups: on Peter himself, on Cornelius, and finally (ch. 11) on the Jerusalem church. So far, we've been experiencing the event through Peter's eyes. Now, in this face-to-face encounter with Cornelius, the stranger to whom God has already spoken, we begin to experience its significance for Cornelius, for those 'outsiders' who lurk on the edges of our religious life, fascinated and yet repelled by what they see inside our churches.

First, Cornelius tells his story in his own words (v. 30). Again, this is a recap of what Luke has already told us, but that bit more vivid: 'Four days ago, about this time, I was praying in my house… and behold!' The wonder of that shining visitor is still with him—along with the incomparable sense of being heard and remembered (v. 31). Cornelius concludes, 'So I did what I was told, and the rest is up to you' (vv. 32–33). As we might expect of a soldier, his words ('commanded', NRSV) have a military feel: he has a sense that both he and his visitor are under orders (compare Luke 7:8).

The God of all

Peter's sermon (the first we've heard outside Jerusalem) is a remarkably vivid evocation of a gospel message that is thoroughly trinitarian, and thoroughly universal. Peter begins with God (vv. 34–35). There is only one God, and that God is (in the old phrase) 'no respecter of persons': he does not discriminate or make distinctions between people on grounds of class, or gender, or race. Peter's rather quaint language here picks up an Old Testament phrase (compare Deuteronomy 10:17); Paul uses similar language in Romans 2:11. It's a familiar phrase, but the force of it is that Peter has suddenly seen what it means for the real person standing in front of him. And that has implications not just for Cornelius but for people of every nation (v. 35).

The Lord of all

What does this God want Peter to say to these people, though? What is the word that Peter has been so elaborately summoned to give them?

'You want a word? Well,' he says, 'I only know one word, the word that God sent to Israel (v. 36), preaching peace through Jesus Christ. Is that what you want to hear?' We can almost hear Peter feeling his way through the broken syntax of his opening sentences. 'Preaching peace' echoes a prophetic phrase (Isaiah 52:7), connected with preaching to the Gentiles in Ephesians 2:17, just as the phrase 'far off' is linked with the worldwide preaching of the gospel in Ephesians 2:13, picking up Joel 2:32 and Isaiah 57:19 (compare Acts 2:39). Whatever God is offering Israel through Jesus, Peter suddenly sees, is offered to all—and that's worth saying, even if he can't yet quite see how the theology works.

So the story of Jesus, the only story Peter knows how to tell, is precisely what needs to be told in this new setting. He can assume that the story is known in outline, even as far off as Caesarea, and verses 37–43 give a good summary of the gospel story. Jesus' ministry comes across as a power struggle between two rival forms of kingship, a mission to rescue those over whom Satan was seeking to exercise illegitimate control (v. 38). But Satan, whatever he may claim, has no right to control any human being, Jew or Gentile: it is Jesus of Nazareth who is 'Lord of all' (v. 36). So the familiar story takes on a new significance. The crucifixion of God's Anointed One (vv. 38–39), the witness of the disciples to his ministry and resurrection (vv. 39–42), the warning of judgment and the offer of forgiveness of sins (vv. 42–43): we have heard all this as a message for Israel, but now we can begin to see that it has a wider, more universal significance. This is a message for the whole world.

The Spirit of all

The result of preaching is (mercifully) in God's hands, not Peter's. The Spirit comes, dramatically and unmistakably, on this group of Gentiles (vv. 46–48), reversing the order of 8:14–17 (where baptism comes first). This is the climax of the episode, the public event which convinces Peter that God is really at work in this unlikely setting (see 11:16).

REFLECTION

'We have to be careful not to fall back into the trap of acting as if the Church were only for people "like us". When in any of our churches people are rejected because "they are not decent" or… because they do not share our political ideology, it is time for us to… ask ourselves what it means to declare that "God shows no partiality".'

Gonzalez 2001, p. 136

36

ACTS 11:1–18

The JERUSALEM CHURCH REFLECTS

'Can anyone withhold the water for baptizing these people?' Peter asks in 10:47. The Ethiopian asks the same question in 8:36, and in both cases it carries a touch of irony. As we see here, there are plenty of people who would like to put barriers in the way of receiving these outsiders into the church. Peter's momentous journey is not finished yet.

Centre and periphery

Back in Jerusalem, rumours are beginning to circulate—either exciting or disquieting, depending on your point of view (vv. 1–2). Where has Peter been all this time? What's going on, out there at the margins, down by the dangerous sea? Is it a time for reasserting centralized control? Or for allowing the margins to change how the centre thinks? Up to this point, 'the church' in Acts has effectively meant the Jerusalem church, with the apostles exercising a regional oversight over the fast-growing bands of believers in Judea and Samaria. Peter and John, in 8:14, act as delegates of the whole body of the Twelve in Jerusalem, acting on behalf of the Jerusalem church as a whole, and it is natural to think that this delegated authority was behind Peter's role when he set out on his journey in 9:32. So this debate is partly about the patterns of authority that direct the ongoing life of the church. Are the apostles answerable to an organization called 'the church', or to someone else?

Why did you do it?

The whole church has heard the news (v. 1); the question comes from one section of that by now large body of believers, 'those of the circumcision' (v. 2). The phrase is odd, given that all believers at this date (apart from Cornelius and his friends) were Jews. It recalls Paul's phrase in Galatians 2:12, and it may be that Luke, looking back on these early discussions, has unconsciously cast them along the party lines of the later debate. What these believers are doing is 'making distinctions'—exactly what the Spirit told Peter not to do in 10:20. But the question is innocent enough, touching on a matter of fact and on a perception that Peter himself had shared (10:28), which must have been troubling more than one of his fellow apostles. Peter has travelled a long way since his rooftop vision in Joppa, but his fellow believers haven't had that experience, so now he needs to lay it before them for a process of joint discernment, retracing his steps and testing every link in that extraordinary chain of events by telling his story 'step by step' (v. 4, NRSV).

Action and reflection

The questioners started with the negative, concerned about rules being broken. But Peter starts with the positive, with the vision of God (v. 5). One approach asks, 'If these are the rules, what does that tell us about God?' The other asks, 'If God is like this, what does that tell us about how we should behave?'

'Take another look at my creation,' says the heavenly voice; 'it's more varied than you think' (vv. 6–7). Peter stresses that his initial reactions were just the same as his hearers': 'I can't, it doesn't make sense, it goes against everything I believe' (vv. 8–10). So Peter needs to hang on to the conviction that it was the voice of God's Spirit, not just a personal whim, that told him to go against God's revelatory word (vv. 12–14). This is not an action that any of us take lightly, and the questioning of our fellow believers will always make us wonder, 'Was I right?' But as Peter retells the story and reflects on it, new connections start to pop up that help to make sense of this new journey led by the Spirit.

Thinking back, the action of the Spirit seen in other people's lives (v. 15; 10:44) is part of what gives Peter confidence that his journey to Caesarea was right—that and the generosity to accord others' spiritual experience equal importance with his own. But only now, reliving the experience with his brothers, does he give us his considered reflection on how it all ties in with the Jesus story (v. 16), the familiar tale now seen with new significance. What this means is nothing less than earth-shaking: it means that the Spirit is not something we earn by keeping the rules, but is God's free gift, for Jew and Gentile alike. And all anyone has to do is to believe in the Lord Jesus Christ (v. 17)—just as the first disciples did. Stop them being baptized? You might as well try to stop God!

REFLECTION

*'Stuckness shouldn't be avoided. It's the psychic predecessor of
all real understanding. An ego-less acceptance of stuckness
is the key to an understanding of all Quality, in mechanical work
as in other endeavours.'*

Pirsig 2000, p. 286

37

A TALE *of* TWO CHURCHES

Meanwhile, the Spirit is busy getting on with things, out there in the world. After the slow-motion ruminations of the Cornelius episode, the pace begins to speed up in this summary section—a reminder of the constant dialectic between reflection and action that characterizes the mature Christian life.

Gossiping the gospel

Back in chapter 8, Luke told us that many of the disciples (probably 'Hellenists', Greek-speaking Jews) were 'scattered' in the persecution that arose after the lynching of Stephen (8:1, 4). It is these anonymous believers who now take the next momentous step in the 'scattering' of God's word. Timing is crucial here: Luke is keeping a number of diverse storylines in play at this point, and it is impossible to be sure of the correlation between the various events in chapters 10—11. From Luke's point of view, however, it is significant that Peter's life-changing encounter with God's Spirit at work in the Gentile Cornelius is placed right in the narrative centre of the book, between the dispersal from Jerusalem and its unexpected harvest—and that the Jerusalem church has accepted the principle of including the Gentiles (11:18) before the next phase begins in earnest.

The distances covered here are huge (v. 19), although it seems probable that many of these Greek-speaking believers (like the Cypriote Barnabas, 4:36) were returning home to their roots. On the way they are 'gossiping the gospel', 'chatting' (NRSV 'spoke') the word. This is mission not as centralized campaign but as real people out on the roads of the empire, sharing the news that is too good to keep to themselves. Initially, the news is shared only with fellow Jews, but some of them, men from Cyprus and north Africa (a long way from home!) come to Antioch and start talking to Greeks as well (v. 20). Imperceptibly, the distinction between Jew and Gentile starts to melt away in cosmopolitan Antioch, and, Luke tells us, 'the hand of the Lord was with them'. This is Pentecost all over again, with 'a large number' believing and turning to the Lord (v. 21; see 4:4; 6:7). The preaching of Jesus as Lord produces exactly the same results as in Jerusalem: against all expectations, this one word that Peter had thought was only for the chosen people allows the Gentiles to discover that they are part of God's kingdom too.

Jerusalem investigates

Word gets back to the church in Jerusalem, already prepared by the events in Caesarea (v. 22). The contact between centre and periphery needs to be kept open, and this time it is Barnabas who is chosen as intermediary. He was a good choice, as it turns out—after all, encouragement is his middle name (4:36)! Barnabas has just the right gifts to nurture this fledgling work of the Spirit: discernment, encouragement and a selfless ability to rejoice at the grace bestowed on others (v. 23). There's an air of gratitude about Luke's report here, and a timely reminder that being 'full of the Spirit' is as much about discerning and nurturing the work of the Spirit in other people as it is about doing the frontline work (v. 24).

Saul joins the team

Verse 25 brings Saul back into Luke's narrative. After his abortive attempt to join the Jerusalem church, he had gone home to Tarsus (9:30). Barnabas, finding himself not too far away, remembers the passionate, fiery young convert, recognizes his potential gifts as a teacher, wonders if he is still in Tarsus, finds him and brings him back to Antioch. This fits in with what Paul says in Galatians 1:21 and with the importance of Barnabas in the early phases of Paul's mission (compare Galatians 2:1, 9). Looking back on those early years, Paul only sees God's hand at work—but God uses human beings to act for him. Bringing Saul to Antioch as a teacher for this fledgling church (v. 26) was a momentous step in the history of the church. What if Barnabas hadn't had his brainwave?

Just in passing, Luke records another significant moment in the life of the church: it is in Antioch that this ever-expanding group of 'disciples' first acquires (probably as a nickname) a distinctive identity. Whose followers are they? Not Saul's or Barnabas's: they are known as *Christianoi*, people who belong to Christ.

PRAYER

Father, help us to rejoice in your gifts to others and to nurture them with love and encouragement.

38 ACTS 11:27—12:23

The APOSTLE & *the* KING

Chapter 12 forms a kind of interlude in a story whose centre is shifting imperceptibly from Peter to Paul, from Jerusalem to Antioch. While Barnabas and Saul are visiting Jerusalem (11:30; 12:25), the focus swings back briefly to Peter and a dramatic prison break.

Spirit-inspired prophecy (11:28) was an important aspect of ministry in the early church, and many of the early prophets were itinerant; Agabus reappears briefly at 21:10–11. Contemporary Roman historians refer to several famines in the eastern Mediterranean in this period, and Luke dates this one to the reign of Claudius (AD41–54). Josephus speaks of a severe famine in Judea in AD46–48. Saul and Barnabas' visit to Jerusalem must belong to the time of the actual famine, not to the time of the prophecy. Luke may not have had precise dates for these long-ago events: more important to his narrative is the lively network of teaching, prophecy and reciprocal charity that continues to link Antioch with Jerusalem.

Herod the king

The Herod of chapter 12 is Agrippa I, the grandson of Herod the Great (the Herod of Matthew 2) and nephew of Herod Antipas, who was ruler of Galilee during Jesus' ministry (Luke 3:1). Agrippa is well known from contemporary Roman and Jewish historians, and the events Luke describes fit the general character of his reign. If the 'precise moment in time' (*kairos*) of 12:1 means the time of the famine (11:28), it would be consistent with the behaviour of despots down the ages to try to deflect attention from ecological disaster by identifying a scapegoat within the population. But there is a chronological problem: the death of Agrippa, which Luke links with Peter's imprisonment, can be dated to AD44, three years into the reign of Claudius but well before the famine described by Josephus in 46–48. Either Luke is thinking of an earlier famine (which is possible), or he has put together separate (undated) items of tradition in a theological rather than chronological sequence.

A miraculous escape

The execution of James is described with stark brevity (12:2), but Peter's imprisonment is told with much more narrative detail and an element of humour. The link with the Passover (12:3–4) explains why Peter was kept in prison: prison in the pre-modern world was normally not a punishment in itself but a holding area pending trial or execution. The problem was (as Paul was to discover: see 24:27) that such 'temporary' custody was outside judicial control and could last indefinitely. All of this, though, is just background to the vivid scene that Luke paints of the apostle in prison, fully expecting to meet the same fate as James, assigned like a dangerous terrorist to four squads of soldiers, chained to his guards—and peacefully sleeping while the church prays for his release (12:4–6). Once again, God's timing gives the story its punch. On the very night before Herod had planned to parade Peter before a hostile crowd, the angel appears and, step by careful step, leads him through mysteriously open doors to the fresh night air of the street (12:7–10).

It's a sensational story: the dazed apostle who doesn't believe what's happening to him; the doors opening 'of their own accord' (12:10); the slave-girl who leaves him knocking at a closed door in the excitement of discovering—beyond all expectations—that God really does answer prayer (12:13–16). God's saving power is always so much greater than we consider possible. Stories like this serve a serious theological function in communities facing the harsh realities of persecution, then and now. Peter's miraculous escape from prison, like Daniel's escape from the den of lions (a favourite theme in early Christian art), provides dramatic demonstration of God's protective power for his persecuted people.

Death of a tyrant

It's also important to know that God does judge evildoers—and that is what Luke shows in the second part of the chapter (compare Daniel 4). There is consternation among the guards at Peter's disappearance, although the fate of the soldiers for their dereliction of duty is anything but funny (12:18–19). Not long afterwards, Agrippa himself comes to a bizarre and gruesome end in Caesarea (12:20–23). Josephus tells a version of the same story, treating Agrippa's death as a fitting punishment for a mortal monarch who accepted the kind of worship due only to God (again, an underlying theme of the Daniel cycle: see Daniel 3).

PRAYER

*Pray for all prisoners and captives… and for those
who have to guard them.*

ACT THREE: PAUL *the* MISSIONARY

This point marks a watershed in Acts, the beginning of a momentous journey which will lead eventually to Rome. The mission now has a new base, Antioch, and a new hero, Saul (aka Paul), who will occupy centre stage in virtually every episode from now to the end of the book.

From Jerusalem to Antioch

First, though, Luke interweaves the different threads of his story with some typically deft narrative footwork. In 12:24 there is a pointed reminder that even the Herods of this world cannot prevent the relentless forward progress of God's saving word. Verse 25 picks up the narrative at the point where we left it at 11:30, with Saul and Barnabas completing their mission in Jerusalem and returning to Antioch with a new team member, John Mark. In passing, Luke tells us that significant changes have been happening in the Jerusalem church. The sudden appearance of 'elders' (11:30), the new role of James the Lord's brother and the departure of Peter to 'another place' (12:17) all raise intriguing questions for the historian. But Luke is not attempting to write a complete history of the early church (or even of all the apostles). His task is to explain the steps by which God's Spirit is preparing the way for the Gentile mission. From this point on, the Jerusalem church is effectively off stage except when Paul revisits the city in chapters 15 and 21.

'The church that was in Antioch'

This formal-sounding phrase (v. 1) recalls the openings of many of Paul's letters, and gives a certain weight and dignity to this fledgling church, which is going to launch the next phase of mission. Suddenly we're in a different world, far more cosmopolitan than Jerusalem. Antioch is a vibrant city which straddles the eastern borders of the Roman empire and controls the trade networks linking east and west. It is appropriate that the church there should be introduced with a certain amount of ceremony. It has its own patterns of ministry: 'prophets and teachers' are mentioned here together for the first time, and (like the Jerusalem church) it has its own leaders, who are carefully introduced by name. Two of these names are familiar: Barnabas, a link back with the apostles and the first, heady days of the Jerusalem church—a trusted, safe pair of hands—and Saul. Three are new: Simeon Niger, a Jewish name with a Latin nickname meaning 'black'; Lucius of Cyrene, another Latin name, pointing to well-established trading and business links between Antioch, Cyprus and north Africa; and Manaen (a Greek form of Menahem), who provides an intriguing link with the Herodian court and a reminder that the Herodian family was also one of the major business empires of the East. 'Herod the tetrarch' is the Herod of the Gospels, a generation back from Agrippa, so Manaen, who had been his youthful companion, must be an older man.

The Spirit's call

It is appropriate too that this next stage in the mission of the church should be marked with spiritual solemnity and ceremony—as in the parallel passage at 6:7–11, which likewise marked the beginning of a new phase in the church's history. Both are formally marked with prayer and the laying on of hands (13:3) in response to the direct guidance of the Holy Spirit, presumably utilizing the prophetic gifts of Antioch's church leaders (13:2). The statement that this happens in the context of worship and fasting gives us a tantalizing glimpse into the spirituality of the early church. The details here all serve to underline that the start of Paul's mission was undertaken within the worshipping life of the church and under the explicit guidance of the Holy Spirit who 'sends them out' (13:4) as they head in a westerly direction, heading initially for Barnabas' old stamping ground—the Jewish communities of Cyprus.

REFLECTION & PRAYER

'For the work to which I have called them' (13:2)—but what work? Sometimes we have to head out in faith, like Abraham, without knowing where God is calling us or what God wants us to do. As a friend said to me when I was ordained, 'Sometimes the Lord leads us into strange places; but where he leads, he always provides.'

MISSION *in* CYPRUS

The journey begins—tentatively at first, following well-trodden pathways, but gradually gaining in confidence and learning to trust God's Holy Spirit. Luke delicately points up parallels between Paul's public ministry and that of his Master, so the first major 'scene' on this voyage shows Paul victorious in conflict with Satan (compare Luke 4:1–13).

Partners in mission

Verse 5 forms a bridge between two sections and sets the pattern for all Paul's missionary journeys. Saul is not yet the leader: he has learnt an immense amount from Barnabas, and the essential pattern of teamwork which undergirds the whole Pauline mission is a pattern set by Barnabas at the start. Their aim is to announce the word of God (not themselves), and their objective is 'the synagogues of the Jews'. In other words, they are using the established networks of Jewish community life in the diaspora. Many Jewish communities did not have dedicated synagogue buildings at this date, but (like the Christians) they did have regular community gatherings, often in people's homes, for prayer and Bible study. The mission on which Saul and Barnabas set out from Antioch was first and foremost a mission to the Jews, a prophetic proclamation of God's word to God's scattered people. True, the church in Antioch (like many Jewish synagogues) has its Gentile adherents as well, and they are starting to find that word relevant to them in unexpected ways, but the full implications of that discovery are still around the corner.

Encounter with a proconsul

We have to assume that Luke's summary sets the general pattern for proclamation throughout the island (v. 6). But now we move to the exceptional event (v. 7), a triangular encounter with rival gurus battling for the soul of the proconsul. Sergius Paulus was the most powerful political figure on the island and the representative of Roman colonial power. Like many high-status Romans of his day, he was clearly fascinated by the battling cults of the eastern Mediterranean, and inspired (by curiosity?) to invite the two representatives of this latest spiritual fad to his residence for a consultation, perhaps to see if there was anything in it for him. Luke notes that he was an intelligent man, and his interest is initially on the intellectual level ('to hear the word', v. 7); but for Elymas (Luke here gives his Greek name, about which there is some confusion) this is a matter of personality control, and he has no intention of losing his position of influence (v. 8). So the word has to be backed up by deeds, and what Sergius Paulus gets is not a reasoned intellectual discourse but a display of spiritual pyrotechnics.

A change of name

Is it coincidence that the Hebrew Saul switches to his Roman name Paulus at this point in the story? Clearly the Roman name was more user-friendly as he began to move west and north, away from the frontier zones and deeper into imperial territory. But Luke also emphasizes the continuity between Saul and Paul. This is the first scene in which we have had a chance to see what has happened to Saul since his own conversion: there are numerous links back to chapter 9, as well as strong verbal parallels with Peter's story. Paul, like the Jerusalem apostles, is 'full of the Holy Spirit' (v. 9) and has that powerful, intent gaze when confronting a spiritual challenge that Peter had at the Gate Beautiful (3:4). The danger with the magical perversion of spiritual power is precisely its power to deceive, the corruption of God-given gifts in the service of spiritual control (v. 10), so it has to be confronted head-on (v. 11).

Perhaps Paul recognized Elymas' opposition to the gospel as a mirror-image of his own self-righteous zeal. Certainly, what Elymas suffers is a parallel to Saul's own experience, a temporary but paralyzing blindness that leaves him groping around for guides. The pro-consul is impressed by the whole package: the 'teaching of the Lord' (v. 12) makes its effect by deed as well as word. There is a dual message here for Luke's first readers: for outsiders, 'Don't mess with these people—they've got the living God on their side'; for insiders, 'Don't get the gospel mixed up with magic'.

FOR DISCUSSION AND PRAYER

This is a disturbing story! Is this the best way to impress the world with the power of the gospel? Or is it the only way to deal with the perversion of the gospel?

ANTIOCH *of* PISIDIA

Travel itself becomes an integral part of the story in Luke's account of Paul's voyages. In this second major scene of the mission, Paul, like Jesus, is offered the opportunity to set out his prophetic vision before an attentive synagogue audience (compare Luke 4:16–30).

Who and where?

Perga in Pamphylia (v. 13) is on the south coast of modern Turkey, one of the few ports of call on this precipitous section of coast, and a major access point for the interior. A paved Roman road, the Via Sebaste, links Perga with Antioch of Pisidia (v. 14), and that is probably how the party reached their next stop. The mission is moving on into unknown territory—although it is worth remembering that Paul was brought up in Tarsus and could have known Antioch as an important staging-post on the trade routes across the interior of Asia Minor. It is also a fact that Antioch was the home town of the proconsul Sergius Paulus, who may well have suggested it to Paul as a strategic base for the evangelization of central Asia Minor (and could have given Paul valuable letters of introduction). The team is gradually changing its focus, too. Luke does not say why John Mark left them at this point (maybe the sight of the mountainous wooded slopes behind Perge put him off!), but the decision will have repercussions later (see 15:37–38).

An impromptu sermon

For Jewish visitors to a strange town, the sabbath-day gathering of the synagogue is the natural meeting-place. Luke assumes that his readers will be familiar with synagogue practice, with the main reading from the Torah followed by a reading from the prophets (v. 15). Paul and Barnabas were probably instantly distinguishable as strangers in town, but may also have been distinguished as visiting scholars from Jerusalem by their dress. A later rabbinic source (Lam.R. 1.1.4) records a saying of R. Huna: 'Wherever a Jerusalemite went in the provinces, they arranged a seat of honour for him to sit upon in order to listen to his wisdom.'

The 'officials of the synagogue' were not rabbis but local benefactors who made major contributions to the fabric of the synagogue and undertook a supervisory role in its meetings. They would be the obvious ones to identify the strangers as scholars and send a message to ask if they have a 'word of encouragement' for the people, linked with the scriptural texts that had just been read. And that is how Paul addresses the congregation, after 'motioning with his hand' (like a Greek orator) to secure their quiet attention (v. 16). They are 'men of Israel', the gathered people of God, no less here than in Jerusalem. There is also an additional element which is going to become increasingly important in the story of Acts: 'you who fear God', the Gentile 'god-fearers' like Cornelius who are attracted to the philosophical purity of Jewish religion and attend sabbath services regularly.

Reclaiming the past

Paul's sermon picks up the history of God's dealings with his people at the point where Stephen's left off in chapter 7, so that for Luke's readers the two together dovetail into a complete account of salvation history. As in Stephen's retelling, Israel's history begins with the action of God (v. 17): election (the choice of a people), divine grace (the Exodus narrative) and exaltation. Note that exaltation is something that happens to God's people 'in exile'—appropriate in an address to a group who are also in some kind of exile. Paul summarizes the years of wilderness wandering and conquest (vv. 18–19), using a patchwork of Old Testament quotations, but his main focus is on God's election of the line of David, heralded by the prophet Samuel (v. 20) and the abortive election of Saul (v. 21). It is David, and the scriptural promises to David, that form the basis of Paul's proclamation here. Jesus, the Saviour who comes of the seed of David 'according to promise', is the culmination of Israel's history (v. 23), with John the Baptist saluted as the forerunner and the final episode in the prophetic witness to the coming of the Christ (vv. 24–25).

FOR DISCUSSION AND PRAYER

What do you see when you look back over history?
Human failure, or divine grace?

42   ACTS 13:26–41

'WE BRING YOU *the* GOOD NEWS'

The prophetic appeal to God's people encapsulated in Isaiah 55 is very much at the heart of what is happening here. When God's word goes forth, we expect a result. God's word never comes back fruitless (Isaiah 55:10–11). The offer is there, and it is totally genuine: living water instead of cracked cisterns, the peace and cosmic rejoicing of God's everlasting covenant (Isaiah 55:12–13). But the prophetic word carries a health warning too. Once it is issued, it must be either accepted or rejected.

You, them, and us

That was then, this is now: in the second part of his sermon, Paul turns from history to the present tense, from God's encounters with his people in the past to the salvation that is on offer now. This synagogue audience is a typical diaspora mixture of Abraham's descendants (ethnically Jewish) and 'those among you who fear God' (emotionally and ideologically Jewish). Paul addresses both as 'my brothers' (v. 26), reciprocating the same warmth of welcome that he has received (13:15). The boundaries of 'brotherhood' in Acts are elastic and fluid: Luke does not limit the term to followers of Christ. The horizons of Paul's message are equally fluid: 'It is to us,' Paul says (pronoun in emphatic position) that 'the word of this salvation has been sent.' Some of our earliest witnesses read 'to you' here (a single letter change in the Greek, which would have sounded identical in dictation)—a reading that picks up the inclusive nature of this appeal: it's for all of us gathered here today, you and me both.

The message of salvation

The words of verse 26 have a distinctly biblical feel without being an exact quotation. God's word here is both judgment and salvation: salvation for those who recognize the fulfilment of God's promise; judgment for those who do not. For Paul, it was not 'the Jews' as a nation who had rejected God's promised Saviour but 'those living in Jerusalem and their rulers'—a very specific group, clearly distinguished from this diaspora congregation (v. 27). But this failure to recognize the Messiah is also a failure to recognize the voice of God in scripture. The Jerusalemites and their rulers thus became the fulfilment of the scriptures that they failed to hear (although Pilate was the actual agent of execution: v. 28). None of this was outside God's control (v. 29; compare 3:17–18), but what happened next was pure grace, pure divine initiative (vv. 30–31).

Witnesses to the people

The role of the witnesses is carefully defined: the witnesses are 'those who came up to Jerusalem with him from Galilee' (v. 31; compare 1:21), and their role is to bear witness to the Jewish people in their homeland. Paul's job is to bring this same good news 'to you' (v. 32), the good news that the promise made to 'our fathers' (13:23) is now fulfilled in God's action in raising Jesus from the dead (v. 33). That's the point of this visit and the fulcrum of the whole sermon. This is not just a piece of abstract history or Bible study: it is about God entrusting his word to his messengers and sending it out to 'you', just as it was earlier sent out to the inhabitants of Jerusalem. Now is your chance; *you* are going to have to decide whether to accept it or to reject it.

The testimony of scripture

This solemn moment of appeal is reinforced by the testimony of scripture. For Luke's readers, this sermon completes the catalogue of testimonies supporting the messianic reading of scripture that runs through all the sermons in Acts, right from chapter 2. Here the focus is appropriately on the two key Davidic texts: Psalm 2 and Psalm 16. What was not fulfilled in David himself comes true in the death and resurrection of David's greater Son (vv. 34–37). What is new here is the link with Isaiah 55:3 (v. 34), linked with Psalm 16:10 by the keyword 'the sure mercies of David'. Finally (and marked by another direct address), the appeal itself: *this* is what I want you to take in, brothers, this is what's in it for you (v. 38). The public proclamation of 'remission of sins' goes back to the roots of the gospel (see Luke 1:77; 3:3), and it is at the heart of the worldwide proclamation, both for Jesus (Luke 24:47) and for Paul (compare Galatians 2:16; Romans 3:28).

REFLECTION

'Your holy hearsay is not evidence.
Give me the good news in the present tense.'

Sidney Carter

43   ACTS 13:42–47

SEEK *the* LORD

Paul's sermon and the sharply polarized reactions to it are described in some detail. This is a paradigmatic scene for the diaspora, just as Peter's sermon in chapter 2 was for Jerusalem. The central event is the proclamation of the word, and we then watch the double helix of belief and unbelief unravelling (just as Simeon predicted in Luke 2:34–35) before our eyes.

Positive reactions

Initial reactions are favourable (v. 42), and many of the congregation, both Jews and 'god-fearing proselytes', throw in their lot with Paul and Barnabas (v. 43). The 'grace of God' is the foundation for the future life of those who become believers (see 1 Corinthians 1:4–9), but Luke is not concerned at this stage with the founding of a new community. What interests him is the wider reaction: on the next sabbath, virtually 'the whole city' (typical Lucan exaggeration!) is agog to hear more of Paul's preaching (v. 44). The 'word of the Lord', which started with John the Baptist's mission to Israel (Luke 3:2), is reaching out to wider and wider circles.

Negative reactions

At this point, however, the insiders react in panic to protect their privileged position (v. 45). 'The Jews' here (as in v. 50) means the unbelievers—possibly the synagogue authorities, certainly those who are not convinced by Paul's arguments and start to argue against his interpretation of scripture (another fulfilment of Simeon's prophecy: see Luke 2:34). 'Jealousy' (NRSV) may be unfair: the Greek word *zelos* can also be translated 'zeal'. Paul's opponents here show the same quality of energetic opposition to God's enemies that he had shown in his preconversion days. Paul uses the same word of himself in Philippians 3:6, so there is no need to imagine that the synagogue authorities were 'jealous' over Paul's success with proselytes or God-fearers. What we have here is a highly coloured and one-sided description of what must actually have happened time and again in Paul's ministry, as he goes 'to the Jew first' (1 Corinthians 9:20; Romans 1:16) and seeks to win over not just a few individuals but a whole community for Christ.

Turning to the Gentiles

This explains, I think, a slight artificiality about the next step, as Paul and Barnabas formally turn on the host community and announce that they have rejected God's prophetic word and judged themselves to be 'unworthy of eternal life' (v. 46). Luke is trying to describe a pattern of formal rejection by Jewish communities in the diaspora, which then justifies Paul's decision to 'turn to the Gentiles'. Rhetorically, this is close to the whole focus of this episode (and therefore of Luke's presentation of the Pauline mission). The word of salvation is sent by God 'to the Jew first'. The Jewish community as a whole has a chance to accept the message (and some do), but the community as a whole rejects it and thus disqualifies itself. So, finally, Paul turns to the Gentiles.

At one level, Luke is defending Paul against the charge of gratuitously abandoning his own people to preach to the Gentiles ('far from it,' he says: 'they pushed me out'). But at a deeper level the whole episode is, like Romans 9—11, a prolonged meditation on the mystery of unbelief which was a fact of life in early Christian experience. Why did Israel not believe? Luke (like Paul) keeps coming back to the problem like a sore tooth (compare especially ch. 28). For the present, the point is made: this is what is happening, and therefore it cannot be outside God's sovereign will (vv. 46, 48). Hence the need to find prophetic warrant, both for the process of rejection and for the alternative mission that begins to open up.

Isaiah 49:6 is a key text in Paul's emergent understanding of his own vocation (v. 47), and links both backwards to Simeon's prophecy and forwards to the end of the book. But note that there is no corresponding turning away *from* Israel. Israel exercises its freedom of choice in rejecting Paul's message, but Paul (as we shall see) keeps returning time and time again to win over the Jewish communities of the diaspora.

REFLECTION

'Pray for those who need to forget the God they do not believe in and meet the God who believes in them.'

Wild Goose, 1999, p. 62

The WORD of GRACE

Inclusion and exclusion are two sides of the same coin. Paul's words signal a new, more positive attitude to Gentiles in his mission, a new recognition that Gentiles are entitled to hear God's word in their own right, not simply to overhear a message addressed to Jews. The expelled word goes out and, as in Luke's parable of the great banquet (Luke 14:15–24), the act of expulsion itself becomes the means of inclusion. Quite what that word will sound like when spoken to Gentiles, though, we have still to hear.

Expelled from Antioch

For the present, the narrative continues to trace the self-destructive spiral of rejection. Preaching to the pagan inhabitants of Antioch proves to be a fruitful experience (v. 48), and the word of the Lord begins to spread outside the city into the surrounding countryside (v. 49). The role of 'women of high standing' (v. 50) fits with what we know of the attraction of highly placed women to Judaism, here used (as often in Roman history) as a short cut to the sources of civic power. Paul and Barnabas are formally escorted across the borders of Antioch. In their turn, they enact the ritual of protest against the city laid down in Jesus' mission commands (Luke 9:5; 10:11) and move on to Iconium (v. 51), leaving behind a small but vigorous cell of disciples, 'filled with joy and Holy Spirit' (v. 52).

On to Iconium

Exactly the same pattern is repeated in Iconium (v. 1)—another indication that the Antioch episode is a type-scene setting the pattern for subsequent mission. Once again, Paul conducts a successful mission in the synagogue, resulting in a mixed crop of Jewish and Gentile believers. Once again, however, he is unable to win over the entire Jewish community to his viewpoint. Not everyone is persuaded, and those who are not stir up hostile feeling against 'the brothers' among the city's Gentile population (v. 2). Mission here is a matter of staying put in a difficult situation as long as one can, doing one's own part in 'speaking boldly for the Lord'—and, much more importantly, watching in awe to see what God is doing (v. 3). As with the

Jerusalem apostles, the mission of Paul and Barnabas is supported and authenticated by the 'signs and wonders' that go along with the faithful proclamation of God's word. The 'word of grace' (and if it isn't that, it isn't the good news of Jesus) is matched by deeds of grace, healing and mending God's broken world.

Division in the city

The scandal of division can't be evaded (v. 4): the whole city is forced to take sides between 'the Jews' and 'the apostles'. This (with 14:14) is the only place where Luke calls Paul and Barnabas apostles. Normally he reserves the term for the Twelve. It may reflect a different source, one with a more distinctively anti-Jewish stance than most of his narrative. Alternatively, it could simply reflect a wider and older usage, in which *apostolos* means 'delegate', as it does in 2 Corinthians 8:23. Paul and Barnabas here are acting as delegates of the church in Antioch from which they were sent out (13:4) and to which they will in due course report back (14:26–27). Eventually, the situation gets out of control (v. 5): the only solution is to recognize the inevitable, move on, and start again (v. 6).

A narrative of exclusion

We need to be very careful when reading texts like this. Luke is not attempting to write a neutral, objective account. Like Paul, he has experienced persecution, and knows at first hand the bitterness of rejection by his own community. Christians in these first generations were always a small, precarious minority, dependent for their survival on the goodwill of the civic authorities. Luke's narrative is designed to instil courage and endurance in communities facing more official persecution. Yet, for us in the 21st century, it is impossible to read these narratives without an awareness of the centuries of Christian ascendancy that reversed the power structures and made Jews, not Christians, a persecuted minority in Europe. Luke could not have imagined the situation that led to the Holocaust, but we have to be careful not to perpetuate any reading of his narrative that demonizes 'the Jews' as the enemies of 'the apostles' and allows Christians to ignore or even support persecution of Jews.

PRAYER

Father, help us to speak your word with grace,
and to meet rejection with love.

MIRACLE *at* LYSTRA

Once again, Luke moves from a generalized summary of Paul's evangelistic activity (vv. 6–7) to a sharply focused, vivid scene that brings the story to life. This episode gives Paul a miracle to match Peter's healing at the temple gate in Jerusalem (ch. 3), and allows us a rare chance to overhear what Paul actually said when he was preaching to Gentile audiences.

Saving faith

Paul is imperceptibly getting deeper and deeper into foreign territory here. Lycaonia (v. 6) is a distinct region of southern Asia Minor, with its own language (v. 11)—not a dialect of Greek—and its own distinctive patterns of religious belief. In Paul's world, the countryside is always a different world from the city, more conservative and less assimilated to the international patterns of Greco-Roman culture. But the man sitting at the town gate of Lystra as Paul and Barnabas approach (v. 8) suffers from a problem that transcends culture. Unable to walk from birth, he is simply classed as *adunatos*, powerless, with no recourse but to sit and watch the world go by, relying on family and passers-by for charitable handouts.

There's nothing wrong with his ears, though, and in fact there's quite a bit of intent listening and watching on both sides here. Paul clearly has the feeling that at least one member of the crowd is really listening (v. 9), and in turn (like Peter at the Gate Beautiful, 3:4) fixes his attention firmly on the one person who has grasped what's on offer in this chance encounter. The good news that Paul brings is all about salvation through faith, and here is one man who longs for healing, wholeness, all that is comprised in the biblical concept of salvation—and clearly has faith that he can find it in Paul's God. That takes faith on Paul's side too. There's no room for whispering in corners here. Paul simply has to shout aloud the offer of resurrection life in Christ: 'Get up and stand straight on your feet' (v. 10).

The gods have come down to earth

Miracles are not self-interpreting: they need a framework of interpretation, and the townspeople naturally call on their own mythology to help them unpack what is going on here. A famous local story tells of the gods Jupiter (Zeus) and Mercury (Hermes) coming down to earth, knocking on door after door and failing to find a welcome, until a humble old couple named Baucis and Philemon open the doors of their cottage and offer them the best of their poverty-stricken fare (Ovid, *Metamorphoses* 8.620–724). Ironically, the crowd here identify Paul, the speaker, as Hermes, the messenger and mouthpiece of the gods, and the quieter Barnabas as Zeus, the king of the gods himself (vv. 11–12). It's a timely reminder that Greek religion has not only its own gods but its own value system, one in which the word plays a much less prominent role than it does in the Bible.

The living God

The joke pales when the apostles suddenly realize what is going on— that the Lystrans are not just using a figure of speech. These pagans understand well that there is only one proper response to the presence of the divine, and that is worship (v. 13). Paul and Barnabas' reaction is swift and dramatic (v. 14). The prophetic action of tearing their clothes arrests the crowd's attention, and holds their attention long enough for Paul to try—somewhat haltingly—to explain why he is so horrified at their totally natural desire to offer sacrifice to these messengers of the divine. The impromptu sermon that follows (vv. 15–17) illustrates the dangers of relying on 'signs and wonders' without a common theological frame of reference. We get a glimpse here of what that frame of reference might look like: a very orthodox condemnation of idolatry based on the appeal to a common humanity (v. 15), a proclamation of good news which does not mention Jesus at all, but concentrates on the living Creator God revealed to 'all the nations' (v. 16) in an outpouring of providence and grace (v. 17).

We shall see in chapter 17 a more fully developed version of Paul's message to the pagan world. Here there is just a hint of judgment (v. 16), but the major emphasis is on the appeal to turn away from idols to serve the living and true God (compare 1 Thessalonians 1:9) who showers us (v. 17) with gifts.

FOR DISCUSSION AND PRAYER

How do we set about preaching the gospel in a post-Christian world which has never read the Bible and does not share our frame of reference?

CLOSING *the* CIRCLE

Lasting results in mission are built not just on the dramatic and miraculous, or even on the heroic and prophetic. Now Paul has to take steps to ensure the survival of the tiny fledgling Christian communities he has planted. In this final section of the first missionary journey, Luke gives us a rare glimpse of Paul in consolidation mode, an essential aspect of his ministry that forms the underlying concern of Paul's own letters.

Death and resurrection

We never get a chance to find out how Paul's sermon went down with its intended audience. The hostility and division that Paul had left behind him in Iconium come back to dog his footsteps (v. 19), and the pagan crowd (crowds are generally fickle in Luke's eyes) is quickly persuaded to abandon its awestruck posture and join in an act of violent expulsion. Being stoned and left for dead is the most violent thing that has happened to Paul so far, and it illustrates how thin is the line that separates adulation from rejection in the sensationalist world of the wonder-worker. Having thrown in his lot with Stephen and the followers of the Persecuted One (9:5), Paul is now really beginning to experience what life is like on the other side of the tracks. But he is not alone: the 'disciples' encircle him (v. 20) in a touching gesture of solidarity and protectiveness, enabling him to get up and walk back into the city that has thrown him out.

Strengthening and encouragement

It is time to move on: first eastwards to Derbe, then back westwards to Lystra, Iconium and Pisidian Antioch (v. 21). Note the sequence of events so economically described in Derbe: preaching the gospel has to be followed by making disciples, the essential next step for survival. These tiny churches cannot rely on their apostolic founders always being there. They have to have the seeds of their own survival built in from the start. Precisely how they survived, here and across the Mediterranean world, is an astonishing story, largely untold, but in the next few verses Luke gives us the essential clues. The task of the itinerant apostles is to strengthen the hearts of the local congregations and encourage them to remain in the faith, and one aspect of this encouragement is the warning that the experience of persecution is built into the job description of being a Christian (v. 22). 'Don't lose heart when this happens,' says Paul; 'I warned you beforehand.' Knowing what to expect is half the battle; and the other half is keeping our eyes on the goal, never losing sight of the glorious vision of what it means to belong to God's kingdom (v. 22).

Patterns of ministry

The other plank in Paul's survival plan for local congregations is strong local leadership. Probably this should be taken as a type-scene for the later missions too. Using the familiar synagogue pattern of a body of 'elders' for each congregation (v. 23), Paul creates a strong dual ministry structure of local elders linked in a network whose mobile agents (as we shall see) are the itinerant apostolic ministers. Fundamental to both, however, is the action of the living God: the one who inspired their loyalty and devotion in the first place is the one to whom Paul can safely commit them for the future.

Back to base

The last few verses of this chapter (vv. 24–28) detail the route that Paul's party takes back home to Antioch in Syria, travelling through Pisidia to Pamphylia, preaching the word in Perga and then dropping down to Attalia (modern Antalya) on the coast. Then it's home to Antioch by the shortest sea-route, back to the community that had 'committed them to the grace to God for the work that they had completed' (v. 26). There's an indescribable sense of achievement in those words. There is nothing quite like the feeling of having launched out in faith, taking the risk of trusting God—and finding that God is with you, opening doors and acting in this world which is God's world (v. 27). It's quite sufficient for a period of rest and rejoicing (v. 28).

PRAYER

'Now to him who by the power at work within us is able to accomplish abundantly far more than all we can ask or imagine, to him be glory in the church and in Christ Jesus to all generations, for ever and ever. Amen.'

Ephesians 3:20–21

CONTROVERSY *at* ANTIOCH

Paul has every reason to relax for a bit: he has a new name, a new vocation, a new mission field. But he's forgotten the folks back home.

The circumcision debate

Just when everything seemed to be going so well—a growing, bustling church in Antioch sending out missionaries in an act of faith, learning to trust the Holy Spirit, planting churches in unexplored territory and discovering a whole new mission field among the Gentiles—controversy rears its ugly head. 'Certain people' (Luke is careful not to give them any kind of official status) come down to Antioch from Judea (v. 1) to say, 'You're doing it all wrong. You can't just bypass the Sinai covenant and sign people up to faith in Jesus—it doesn't make sense. God has revealed once for all in the scriptures the means of salvation. How can you just set it aside?'

It is important to listen to both sides of this controversy. We get a slightly different perspective in Galatians 2, which gives us Paul's personal view on the controversy at the time it was all happening. There is a long and complicated scholarly debate over the relationship between Luke's account of the apostolic council here and the events described in Galatians. It is actually quite difficult to reconcile the two accounts, and it seems most likely that Luke, writing some 40 years later, didn't have access to precise timings (who would remember all this after the protagonists had all passed on?), and has conflated two events to give a general impression of the way the controversy worked. Either way, Paul's letter gives us a very good idea of the way the controversy blew up, and of what Paul himself would have said to justify his own position (Galatians 2:15–20).

What's at stake?

The other side in the debate has a theological viewpoint too, however—a viewpoint based on fidelity to God's revealed word in scripture. This is the viewpoint represented by Peter's anguished and tentative deliberations over the call to meet Cornelius in chapter 10 —the beginning of the story to which this chapter effectively forms the coda. In fact, Paul doesn't get a chance to speak in Luke's version of the story: it is Peter who has the decisive word, as we shall see. And it is important for us, reading the story now as 21st-century Christians, to be prepared to hear both sides. It is much too easy to dismiss Paul's opponents as 'the Judaizers' or 'the circumcision party', as if the problem was all to do with 'them' and not 'us'. At one level, this controversy is about holiness—about what it means to be living as God's called and chosen people in God's world. More broadly, we could see it as a debate about inclusion and exclusion, about the terms on which we are prepared to welcome strangers into our religious communities. Do they have to change to become like us, or are we prepared to let them change the nature of our community? This is not simply a controversy from the past, but one that is reflected time and time again in the history of God's people—not least in current controversies over sexuality or medical ethics. All of us, Jew and Christian alike, have to wrestle continually with the tension between law and grace, between preserving the tradition and moving forward in the Spirit, between God's revealed will in scripture and the work of the Spirit in God's world.

Argument and debate

Acts 15 is also about how to deal with dissension and debate within God's people, about how the church acts to tackle a potentially destructive conflict. Jerusalem here assumes, for the first time in Acts, a mediatorial role, with both sides sending delegates to argue their case before the apostles and (also for the first time) the elders of the Jerusalem church, assuming implicitly the role of the Sanhedrin as an arbiter and repository of traditional wisdom in Jewish society. The delegates' route through Phoenicia and Samaria (v. 3) assumes the character of a triumphal procession, giving Paul and Barnabas an opportunity to relate the conversion of the Gentiles to the Christian communities all along the road.

REFLECTION

'The story begins with the experience of two individuals and expands step-by-step into a debate and decision of the church as a whole. In the process, the church discovers new dimensions of what "we believe".'

Johnson, 1996, p. 107

The APOSTOLIC COUNCIL

It's easy for the old, traditional centres in church life to think they have all the answers, and for those who have traditionally been recipients of 'mission' to think they have nothing to contribute. This passage encourages both sides to see matters in a different light.

Learning to listen

Listening is essential to any genuine process of trying to discern God's will, and there is a remarkable amount of both listening and silence going on in this passage—but that takes time to establish. The first step is a warm welcome (v. 4) from the whole church in Jerusalem, giving Paul and Barnabas the opportunity to tell their story, together with their own reflection on it. It is about what God has been doing (not about what the missionaries have been doing) among the Gentiles. The first reaction to his account, though, is negative (v. 5): bringing in Gentile converts is fine, but they have to be real converts. In other words, they have to be circumcised and keep the Mosaic law. Note that this is not a dispute between insiders and outsiders but between fellow Christians with different views of what it actually means to make a commitment to Christ.

Peter's testimony

The next step is to convene a formal apostolic conclave of the apostles and elders (v. 6) to discuss the matter. The first impression is nothing but a confused noise of argument and debate (v. 7). The key to unlocking the whole sterile controversy and moving it forward lies in Peter's willingness to give his own testimony. Being willing to stand up and say 'I was wrong' testifies to a rare breed of courage and honesty in a church leader. God is the subject of all the verbs in these opening verses: it was God who chose Peter to speak to the Gentiles (v. 7); it was God who gave the Gentiles the visible testimony of the Spirit 'just as to us' (v. 8); it was God who 'made no distinction between us and them', cleansing their hearts through faith (v. 9). Here we are right back in Cornelius' front parlour, watching with bated breath as God's action in sending the gift of the Spirit (10:44) confirms Peter's internal hunch that it was right to go with the strangers, right to cross over into their territory.

It is only now, though, that we can hear Peter making the final theological connection between his vision of clean and unclean animals (10:11–15) and the visit to Cornelius. How did God 'cleanse' the Gentiles' hearts? Not by righteous deeds (which is what we might have expected from 10:35) but by faith—'just it was as for us' (v. 9). Here we have proof that God does not discriminate between Jews and Gentiles. How do we know? Because of the gift of the Spirit. And because of that visible gift, we can make deductions about the invisible inner person, the 'heart' that only God sees (v. 8). This same fundamental point of God's refusal to discriminate underlies verse 11: we believe that salvation comes through the grace of the Lord Jesus, and so do they.

The yoke of the commandments

The practical conclusion comes in verse 10, with a direct appeal to the assembly: 'Why do you put God to the test?' This is emotive language reminiscent of Gamaliel's appeal to the Sanhedrin (5:39), and it expresses one of the central dilemmas of Acts. Are we capable of discerning the new things that God is doing, or are we so determined on maintaining our own loyalty to past ways of interpreting God's will that we end up fighting against God? The issue here, though, is a practical one: what are Gentiles committed to when they enter the community of the Messiah? In traditional Jewish thought, accepting circumcision meant (gladly and willingly) 'taking on oneself the yoke of the commandments', that is, taking up Israel's privilege of trying to keep the whole of God's law. But, says Peter, this is a yoke that neither we nor our fathers were able to shoulder, so why put it on the necks of Gentile believers?

REFLECTION

'The place where we are, at this apparent edge, is where God is doing new things. And those who daily see the new things that God is doing in the world have the obligation toward God and toward the rest of the Christian world to go back to the old centers, which often have lost much of their vision, taking to them our renewed vision of what God is doing today.'

Gonzalez 2001, pp. 179–80

JAMES INTERVENES

Testimony and silence go together in this delicate debate. Peter's testimony creates the silence that finally allows the testimony of Paul and Barnabas to be heard (v. 12). Then it's their turn to be silent to hear a new voice (v. 13).

James of Jerusalem

James has not been properly introduced up to now in Acts (apart from the brief note in 12:17), and even now Luke seems to assume that his readers will know who he is. He is one of the brothers of the Lord mentioned briefly at 1:14, and has clearly come to play an important role in the Jerusalem church. It is typical of Luke's lack of interest in church governance that he does not trouble to explain what has been going on in the Jerusalem church while the narrative focus has been on Antioch and Paul's mission. Paul calls James one of the 'so-called pillars' of the Jerusalem church (Galatians 2:6–9) and believes that the troublemakers of Galatians 2:12 came from James (although James denies this in Acts 15:24, or at least implies that they had exceeded their brief). Later tradition makes James the first bishop of Jerusalem, but the letter issued by the council and the decision it records (vv. 22, 23) come from the group, not from the individual.

An authority of listening

What is important about James is that he has the moral authority to comment on what has been happening and to command the attention of the whole assembly (v. 13). It is an authority based first of all on listening. James has been silent all this time, listening to Peter's account of his experience in Caesarea (15:7–11), and listening to Paul and Barnabas (v. 12), the centre being prepared to listen to what is going on at the margins. Within those stories, there is a process of listening to God, discerning the signs that God is at work in unexpected ways and places.

For James, the point that emerges most clearly from Peter's story is 'first God' (v. 14): God's action out there in the world comes first. It seems clear that James is referring to Peter's story here, using formal, biblical-sounding language that echoes God's original choice of his people from among the nations of the world in such Old Testament passages as Deuteronomy 14:2 (compare Exodus 19:5; 23:22; Deuteronomy 7:6). The verb *epeskepsato* (NRSV 'looked favourably') is the same as that used in the Benedictus at Luke 1:68, 78, and conveys the sense of 'God's decisive, liberating action on behalf of the persons concerned' (Barrett 1998, p. 724). What happened in Caesarea, James implies, is the liberation of a new people as exciting and dramatic as the exodus story, and it is happening before your very eyes.

The authority of scripture

The second essential component in James' authority is his ability to listen to the word of God in scripture and to discern how the 'this' of God's action now corresponds to the 'that' of the prophetic witness. Theological discernment means holding together the new and the old, the action of the living Spirit with the revealed words of the eternal God (v. 15). The passage James chooses to provide the scriptural warrant for the Gentile mission (vv. 16–17) is from Amos 9:11–12. It is not the most obvious one to our way of thinking, and the argument depends on the ancient Greek translation of the Hebrew Bible. Jewish biblical scholars believed that only the consonantal text of the Hebrew Bible was inspired, so in Hebrew it is easy to read 'the remnant of Edom' (Amos 9:12, NRSV) as 'the rest of humanity' (reading Adam in place of Edom). That gives us the sense 'all other peoples' (Acts 15:17, NRSV), a minimal verbal alteration of the Hebrew that completely reverses the sense of the text. In the Greek Bible, 'humanity' becomes the subject of the sentence instead of its object, so that the text becomes a prophecy of the Gentiles 'seeking the Lord'. This passage probably formed part of an early Christian collection of *testimonia* or proof-texts. James uses the exegetical techniques of his own day in the service of an apostolic fidelity to God's revelation to the past that includes adaptation to God's revelation in the present.

REFLECTION

'The basic decision, after all, is to let God be God, to say "yes" to the work of the Lord, which goes before the church's ability to understand or even perceive it.'

Johnson, 1996, p. 107

The APOSTOLIC DECREE

James' solution is a neat compromise. Gentile Christians do not need to be circumcised, and are not bound to keep the whole Mosaic law (vv. 19, 28). Note that this is a ruling *for Gentile Christians* (v. 23). There is nothing in it to prevent Jewish Christians from continuing to keep the law if they so desire; in fact, that is almost certainly James' unexpressed premise. But this does not mean that Gentile believers are under no moral constraints at all—heaven forbid! (as Paul would have said: Romans 6:2). In fact, all the New Testament epistles seek in a variety of ways to define the moral code under which Christians now live. They are subject to the 'law of Christ', which means the law of love (Romans 13:8; 1 Corinthians 13; Galatians 5:14; 6:2)—and, as Paul shows in Romans 14 and 1 Corinthians 8 to 10, one of the things that this means is prioritizing the needs of my brother or sister in Christ above my own 'rights' to express my freedom in Christ.

James' solution seems to focus on this area, the area thrown into relief by the Antioch controversy (Galatians 2) and hinted at in Acts 11:1–10: that is, the very practical issue of maintaining table-fellowship between two different groups of Christians living by different dietary regulations.

The Noahide laws

There are two suggestions as to what precisely is meant by the restrictions proposed by James (v. 20) and circulated in the apostolic decree (v. 29). One is that this is a version of the moral laws which, in Jewish tradition, were part of God's covenant with Noah and his descendants after the flood (Genesis 9:1–17). Jewish thinkers regarded these as constituting a basic 'natural law' binding on all humanity. The traditional number of the Noahide laws is seven, but contemporary lists vary from three to 30, focusing on the core areas of idolatry, sexual immorality and bloodshed. 'Pollutions of idols' (v. 20) is a more general term for impurity derived from contact with pagan worship, and is glossed more specifically as 'idol-foods' at verse 29 (compare also 21:25): that is, food that has been sacrificed to a pagan deity. This was the most likely form in which Jews or Christians might come into contact with this form of impurity.

The law of the alien

The other possibility is that the list is derived from the prohibitions binding on 'the alien who sojourns among you' in Leviticus 17—18, which includes these three with the addition of 'things strangled'. This fourth prohibition ties the restrictions more closely to the dietary restrictions of observant Jews, and makes it easier to read 'from blood' as a dietary rather than a moral restriction. This would fit in with the Antioch incident as described in Galatians 2:11–14, and could be seen as a move designed to make it easier to maintain table-fellowship between Gentile and Jewish believers. But some early manuscripts omit this clause and add in its place a negative version of the Golden Rule ('And not to do to others whatever they do not wish to be done to them'). This turns the list more obviously into a list of fundamental ethical rules, with 'blood' meaning 'bloodshed'—that is, murder.

The council decrees

James gives his considered opinion (v. 19), but it is the whole assembly—the apostles and elders plus the whole church—who make the final decision (v. 22). Luke uses the language of a formal civic decree, familiar from countless inscriptions and imperial edicts across the Mediterranean world. The decree is then translated into a formal letter (vv. 22–23), sent back with Paul and Barnabas and two official delegates from Jerusalem to the church in Antioch which had requested a ruling, and to 'the brothers in Syria and Cilicia' (v. 23, Paul's home province). The letter throws a fascinating light on the processes of decision making in the early church: the decision is the result of a formal conclave and has the seal of the Holy Spirit (v. 28). It gives an implied reprimand to the unauthorized zealots who were trying to impose unnecessary restrictions on new converts, and gives a formal seal of approval to Paul's mission (vv. 25–26).

FOR DISCUSSION AND PRAYER

What happens when the needs of Christian fellowship seem to conflict with Christian freedom—or with the desire to impose a strict moral code on new believers?

PAUL *the* MISSIONARY: PHASE TWO

This episode marks a decisive break for Paul in more ways than one, and changes his relationship both with Antioch and with Jerusalem. He returns to Antioch with two new colleagues and an endorsement of the Gentile mission initiated by the church in Antioch, but his own vision embraces wider horizons.

Mission accomplished

The immediate task is to take back the council's decision to Antioch, where the problem first arose. A formal meeting of the body of believers is convened (v. 30), and the decision is received with joy as an affirmation of this frontline church's sense of the Spirit's leading (v. 31). Judas and Silas (v. 32) were clearly well chosen for their task of mediating between the centre and the margins—congenial to the believers in Antioch, equally open to the Spirit, and able to encourage and strengthen the church. There is some confusion in the manuscripts about the Jerusalem delegates' return to base (vv. 33–34): did they both go back? If so, how did Silas come to be available for Paul's next mission (v. 40)? Luke is notoriously vague about chronology, and the periods covered in verses 33–36 may be a matter of months rather than days.

A break with Barnabas

The initial result of the delegation to Jerusalem is a period of affirmation and consolidation in Antioch (v. 35), but Paul's restless vocation will not leave him content to stay in one place for long. He has not forgotten the fledgling communities that sprang into being on his first missionary excursion (v. 36).

First, though, Paul breaks with his long-standing friend and mentor Barnabas (vv. 37–39). This must have been painful: verse 39 uses strong language indicating profound irritation or exasperation. The immediate cause was poor John Mark, Barnabas' cousin (as we discover from Colossians 4:10), the young man who had left them at the beginning of the journey to Pamphylia (13:13). Did Paul feel this desertion as a lack of personal loyalty? Or did he simply doubt John Mark's roadworthiness for another long trip? Luke does not tell us, but the split must have been significant for him to mention it at all. This is the last time Barnabas appears in the story of Acts, although he is mentioned affectionately by Paul in 1 Corinthians 9:6. John Mark's tracks reappear at intervals across the later Pauline letters (see Colossians 4:10; 2 Timothy 4:11; Philemon 24) and also at 1 Peter 5:13. Later tradition treats him as Peter's companion and secretary in Rome.

A new team

The split with Barnabas heralds the first steps towards building a new team. Paul's vision of ministry was always collaborative, and we can see from his letters that he has an astonishing capacity to deploy a complex team of delegates from a constantly mobile base. Two of the new team who meet us in the later epistles are introduced here. Silas (vv. 32, 40) is almost certainly the same as Paul's later companion Silvanus: Paul always uses the Latin form of his name, Luke the Greek. He will be Paul's major partner in the next phase of his mission (see 2 Corinthians 1:19; 1 Thessalonians 1:1; 2 Thessalonians 1:1).

Timothy (vv. 1–3) is different. Hand-picked from among the first-fruits of the first mission, the son of a mixed marriage, this is a young man who has already shown his survival capacity in the testing conditions of the frontier church in Lystra. Timothy's mother (Eunice), along with his grandmother Lois, are described in 2 Timothy 1:5 as women of faith—the same characteristic that Luke singles out here (v. 1). As a Jewish woman married to a Greek, Eunice is rather typical of the earliest Christian converts: belonging by faith and heritage to the Jewish community, but marginalized by marrying out. Timothy is one of the first 'second generation' converts of the new faith, a welcome sign that discipleship can pass from one generation to another (2 Timothy 3:15). Having a Jewish mother, Timothy was legally Jewish, so Paul's decision to circumcise him (v. 3) is perfectly consistent with Paul's own policy in 1 Corinthians 9:20, and equally with the decision not to circumcise Titus (Galatians 2:3), who was not Jewish.

PRAYER

When we fail you, Lord, help us not to despair. Give us the confidence to come back to your love and the humility to pick ourselves up and try again.

52

The ROADS NOT TAKEN

It's not always easy when the Spirit says 'No', especially when we are busting with new ideas, new projects, new glimpses of great works to do for God. But Paul and his party need time for foundation-laying: travelling together, learning to trust one another, learning to trust God and to seek God's direction together.

An episcopal visitation

From this point on, Paul becomes more and more a freelance operator, learning to trust the Spirit for himself, but increasingly divorced from HQ. Back home in Antioch, all his friends can do is to entrust him to God's grace (15:40). The new journey begins as a pastoral visit to the churches founded on the first missionary journey in chapters 13—14. Paul's vision of the apostolic office already includes a commitment to 'oversight' (15:36), the continuing duty to care for an ever-expanding flock that was to take up so much of Paul's energies in the years to come. He finds the congregations flourishing, growing both in numbers and in the strength of their faith (v. 5). Paul takes the land route this time, up through northern Syria and Cilicia, then through the mountain passes of the Taurus to link up with the Via Sebaste leading westwards towards Asia. Was this area included in the 'Cilicia' of the apostolic decree (15:23)? Paul clearly considers it part of his brief to convey the decisions of the apostolic council to this region as well (v. 4).

A change of plan

So far, so good; but Paul has no intention of stopping there. The Lycaonian-speaking population of Lystra had been temporarily impressed by the miracle of 14:8–18, but there was not much scope for sustained evangelization in the non-Greek villages of these upland areas. Paul's natural route would have been to make directly for the prosperous Greek cities of the Aegean coast and to open up the Roman province of Asia for the gospel. But, at a fork in the road (probably somewhere around Antioch of Pisidia), a fateful decision is taken and the party decides to head north, not west (v. 6).

Galatia was a huge province which included Lycaonia and the

cities of Derbe, Lystra, Iconium and Antioch in its southern region. Phrygia (technically within the province of Asia) lies along its western border. The old trade route through Antioch runs north through Phrygia towards Bithynia and the populous Greek settlements of the Black Sea coast (v. 7). But again, the Spirit says 'No'; so, cutting down past the mountainous region of Mysia, the puzzled and frustrated little party find themselves in the busy port of Alexandria Troas, the natural embarkation point for crossing over into Europe (v. 8).

Journeying with the Spirit

By the time they get to Troas, Paul and his party have travelled almost as far north as they will travel south in chapters 16—18. Was this all a completely fruitless journey? Not entirely: next time Paul passes this way, there will be 'disciples' to be strengthened and to offer fellowship, both in Phrygia and Galatia (18:23) and in Troas (20:6–12). Wherever Paul travels, the seed is sown, one way or another. Nevertheless, there is a mounting sense of frustration in this journey as the Spirit balks Paul's plans in one place after another. Ever since his acrimonious split with Barnabas, there is a sense that Paul is striking out on his own, moving into a territory without signposts. This mission, unlike the first, is not planned and directed by the home church. Nevertheless, Luke makes it very plain that the whole journey is under the guidance of the Holy Spirit (who is also the 'Spirit of Jesus', vv. 6, 7).

Silas, we should not forget, had prophetic gifts, as did Paul himself. And the final step, too, there in the harbour town backed by Mount Ida, where the only way out is by sea, comes as the result of a revelatory vision in which Paul sees a man from Macedonia pleading for help (v. 9). It is a dream shared with his companions: verse 10 shows that this is a team decision, based on a team discernment. It's the clue the party has been waiting for. Finally, after all the 'No's, there is an unambiguous 'Yes'. It's time to take to the sea.

FOR DISCUSSION AND PRAYER

How do we look for the guidance of the Spirit in our own journey (or as a church)?

A SELLER *of* PURPLE DYE

The 'we concluded' of 16:10 tells us that the team has acquired a new member—either Luke himself or somebody whose diary he had access to. Either way, there is a new vividness and immediacy about the next phase of the story, especially in relation to travel.

Over to Macedonia

The party's new diarist speaks like a businesslike and experienced traveller, someone who knows his way around the shipping routes of the Mediterranean seaboard and relishes the circumstantial details of the journey. The first leg of this new phase of the journey is by sea over to the island of Samothrace, then across the Saronic Gulf to Neapolis (New City) on the Macedonian coast (v. 11). Then it's back to the Roman road—a relief, probably, after trekking across the high plateaux of Anatolia—a road with a sense of direction. The Via Egnatia led from the Aegean coast straight across Macedonia to the ports of the Adriatic, and then to Brundisium (Brindisi) and Rome. It was the obvious route to follow into this new territory, and it leads straight to Philippi, a city with a strong sense of its own importance and of its place in the imperial economy.

Luke tells us that Philippi was a colony (v. 12), a little bit of Rome on Macedonian soil, populated by civil war veterans from the Roman army and imbued with a distinctively Roman identity. It must have presented a distinctive challenge to Paul, faced with a blank wall of imperial indifference and a gratuitous display of Roman military power, very different from the cosmopolitan eastern cities of Tarsus and Jerusalem or from the remote upland villages of the Anatolian plateau. But all roads lead to Rome, and the milestones along the Via Egnatia would make it clear just how close the city was getting—no further, overland, than Paul had already travelled from Antioch. Was this where Paul first began to form his desire to see Rome (19:21)? Perhaps, but he is certainly not going to get there by the direct route.

The women by the river

The party spend a few days in the city (v. 12), looking for an entrée. Paul's usual strategy of connecting with the local Jewish community is frustrated by the fact that he cannot find a synagogue. Perhaps the community was too small to have its own meeting place, or perhaps the Roman magistrates here were strict in applying to this little bit of Rome the rules enforced in the capital, which at this period forbade the cultivation of foreign worship within the city boundary. That makes it difficult to engage in public evangelism, too: you can't just turn up in an ancient city and take over the streets. Outside the city walls, however, on the banks of the river that provided running water for ritual baths, they find a group of women assembling for prayer on the sabbath (v. 13), and there a series of informal conversations bear their first fruit. Paul's strategy is based on finding common ground, sitting down and talking—not megaphone evangelism, but 'gossiping the gospel'.

A house church is born

Lydia (v. 14) in many ways epitomizes the profile of these early Pauline communities. She is an independent businesswoman, obviously mistress of her own household and able to offer hospitality to a group of visiting scholars. Like dyers everywhere, she will tend to base her business by the riverside, on the city's margins, and in Philippi she is doubly marginalized. As an immigrant from Thyatira in a Roman city (and a woman into the bargain) she will be tolerated and taxed but hardly integrated into the civic life of the colony. As a god-fearer or 'worshipper of God', she will be similarly tolerated but not fully integrated into the life of the small Jewish community. Nevertheless—perhaps because of this marginality—she is receptive to the gospel and becomes the founding member of a new community, baptized along with her entire household (v. 15). Her house, hospitably offered as a base for Paul's operations, becomes the nucleus of the new house church. Hospitality was and remained the key to the establishment of church life in the cities of the empire. Patrons like Lydia offered a vital service to the church, not only through making physical space available for the church to meet in but also by offering some kind of political protection. The next episode, though, will make it clear how very precarious their position is.

PRAYER
Father, we thank you for Lydia, and for all who offer their homes
as a base for the work of the gospel.

EXORCISM & ARREST

In the unfolding story, the narrator and his readers see the whole picture, and have a broad idea of what is going on. If these Bible stories are familiar, it's even easier for us to take each development for granted, to see it as inevitable. But none of the characters inside the story has that privileged knowledge, and in real life we are the characters, not the narrator. A dramatic story like this is a good opportunity for an exercise in empathy: pick one of the characters and try to get under their skin. Then read the story again, slowly, and try to experience it from the point of view of your character. Forget what everybody else (including the reader) knows: just think about what your character knows.

The slave-girl

The slave-girl is even more marginalized than Lydia. She doesn't even have a name. She is just a female slave (v. 16) with a gift for divination—somebody who would probably be classed as mentally ill in modern Western society, but with a distinct potential for commercial exploitation. A 'Python' spirit is a spirit like the famous prophetic spirit that inspired the priestesses of Apollo at the Delphic oracle. Luke takes it for granted that such spirits exist and have their place in the divine economy. As with the demon-possessed people in the Gospels, everything the girl says of Paul and his companions is true (v. 17), though couched in terms that make sense in a pagan environment. Numerous inscriptions from this area make it clear that devotion to 'God Most High' was common in this area, possibly as a result of Jewish influence. So what we have, in this unlikely form, is a prophetic message from the local divinities to the people of Philippi—and the message is that the gospel-gossip that Paul is sharing with the Jewish women at the riverside is a 'way of salvation' for the whole city.

The missionary

To Paul and his party, the slave-girl and her owners are initially just part of the colourful crowd of market vendors milling around the narrow streets leading out of the forum and impeding their way through to the river-gate. But somehow she's always there, following Paul and shouting after him, day after day: it's getting embarrassing (vv. 17–18). Of course,

Paul could have taken her prophecy as an unsolicited testimonial and exploited it for his own ends, but that would be to treat her the same way as her masters do. Instead, he treats her the way Jesus did—as a real person who deserves to have control of her own life (v. 18).

The slave owners

To the slave owners, this is a gratuitous act of commercial vandalism. Slaves in ancient law were chattels—'living tools', as the Greek philosopher Aristotle put it—possessed of certain physical or mental skills which could be used at will by their owners. And this was a pretty profitable one, a nice little earner, suddenly gone without trace. Looking into her eyes, they knew that they would never be able to manipulate her in quite the same way again. Their response is that nothing must be allowed to stand in the way of business interests (v. 19).

The magistrates

It's not too difficult for the slave's owners to exploit Paul's precarious position as a Jew in a Roman city (vv. 20–21), and magistrates and crowd readily concur (v. 22). In the Roman empire, you could preach what you liked as long as it didn't interfere with trade: then it became political. There is a certain irony in the fact that Paul and Silas are accused of teaching unlawful Jewish customs (vv. 20–21), a charge that Paul makes no attempt to deny. Jews were allowed to practise their own religion as long as they did not try to proselytize others. Because it was not comfortably polytheistic like most religions, Judaism was seen as antisocial by contemporary Roman writers: being Jewish (or Christian) meant detaching yourself from the normal civic religious practices of the empire, and that was always seen as dangerous. The punishment is being 'beaten with rods' (v. 22), a technical term for corporal punishment administered by Roman magistrates. Paul uses the same term at 2 Corinthians 11:25. Throwing them into jail (v. 24) is simply a way of asserting control, making sure they can't continue to peddle this mischievous superstition.

REFLECTION

Believing in God is OK as an add-on, as long as it doesn't interfere with the rest of my life, or with business, or with politics. Where have we heard that one before? What modern parallels can you think of for the characters in this story?

55   ACTS 16:24-40

PRISON & EARTHQUAKE

Most Westerners take for granted the freedom to travel around the world on business or holiday trips, but many non-Westerners could tell us that international travel is a very different experience if you have the wrong kind of passport—or the wrong colour skin.

Paul the prisoner

Becoming a victim of the Roman judicial system was no joke. Paul and Silas are stripped of all human dignity, manacled to a beam in the innermost cells—hot, foetid, dark and smelly (v. 24). Finding the ability to pray in this situation (v. 25) is a mark of spiritual maturity. Having taken the step of faith, crossed over to Europe after that long fruitless trip north and made one convert, most of us would want to ask, 'Where is God in all this?' Yet Paul and Silas find the courage not only to pray (privately, desperately, silently) but to sing hymns—an act of public fellowship and defiance that reaches the ears of the jailer. Feeling the first tremors of an earthquake must have seemed at first like the last straw to the prisoners trapped in that airless cell (v. 26). But it is (literally!) an act of God, revealing God's presence in no uncertain terms, leaving the doors gaping open and the manacles broken. The messengers of the gospel can't be so easily constrained: there is a greater power than the emperor's at work here.

The jailer

We already know that the jailer is a conscientious town official, taking extra care to keep his prisoners safe in the innermost cells. Those special orders must mean that these prisoners must not be allowed to escape at any cost. So his first thought, on being jerked out of sleep by the earthquake, is that he has failed in his charge: the doors are open and the prisoners must have escaped (v. 27). Paul, though, has more at stake than his own personal safety. The jailer is not just a political symbol but a real person poised between disaster and salvation (v. 28), and Paul's intervention brings him back from despair to a glimpse of hope (v. 30). So the jailer, calling for light to illuminate that black pit of despair, becomes a paradigm for the readers' response to Luke's story, moving from despair and guilt to fearful trembling at the revelation of divine grace (v. 29), then to faith, to salvation, to baptism into a new community (vv. 30–33). Finding the light of grace in the pit of darkness rebuilds the bonds of humanity between the jailer and his charges. As he washes the prisoners' wounds, takes them home and puts a meal in front of them, his whole household is suffused with joy (v. 34). So when, in the morning, word comes down that Paul and Silas are to be released, the jailer's relationship with his prisoners is totally transformed (v. 36).

Let these men go

This was Paul's first real experience of being on the wrong side of the Roman legal system. To a Roman citizen on the road, Rome represented peace and stability, good roads and protection for travellers. But here in Philippi, Paul experiences Roman power from the underside, and it's not a happy experience. So when the magistrates, having left their prisoners to cool their heads overnight, send word to let them go, the curt formal message (v. 35) is met with a surprising refusal (v. 37). Paul is acutely conscious of the public degradation he has suffered, and is determined to reverse it. He is not an object but a person, someone with a status that should actually mean something in the Roman world (v. 38), and especially in Philippi, where citizenship meant being 'Roman' in a particularly conscious way (see 16:21). As countless prisoners have found, the only answer to the attempt to dehumanize is to refuse to allow it: the dogged assertion of human worth is an essential response to tyranny in any form. So Paul leaves Philippi (v. 40), but on his own terms (v. 39) and after re-establishing contact with Lydia and the little group of 'brothers' (which must include sisters!)—the marginal group in that Roman colony which has the only citizenship that really matters (compare Philippians 3:20).

PRAYER

'Where can I go from your spirit? Or where can I flee from your presence? If I ascend to heaven, you are there; if I make my bed in Sheol, you are there… If I say, 'Surely the darkness shall cover me, and the light around me become night', even the darkness is not dark to you; the night is as bright as the day.'

Psalm 139:7–8, 11–12

56

ANATOMY *of a* RIOT

Paul's missionary odyssey unfolds in a series of vivid vignettes, strung along the relentless plod of the journey. Luke's narrative gives little feeling for the passing countryside but conveys a strong sense of the road itself.

To Thessalonica

The next two staging-posts, Amphipolis and Apollonia, pass without incident. Paul's goal is Thessalonica, an ancient port city with a flourishing commercial centre. Here, there is a strongly established Jewish community with its own 'synagogue' (NRSV) or 'assembly' (v. 1)—not necessarily a building, but a formal weekly meeting for prayer and study of the scriptures. This is Luke's clearest statement yet that it was Paul's custom to attend the synagogue (v. 2), using the sabbath community gatherings as the obvious forum to expound his message (v. 3).

The crucified Messiah

There are twin strands to Paul's preaching (v. 3): it is grounded in scripture ('it was necessary'—that is, part of the divine plan), and it is based on personal experience ('this Jesus whom I proclaim to you'). It's the second strand that brings the message alive, with an unexpected slide into the first person. And the focus of the message itself has begun to shift. The bone of contention, the double helix that has to be held together at all costs, is the Messiah who both suffered and was raised from the dead. The magnetic centre of Paul's preaching is the crucified-and-risen one, the Jesus who suffered an ignominious death on the cross: this is the 'this' for which he has to find a 'that' in the scriptures. What texts he used, Luke does not tell us. Perhaps he expects us to remember the key text from Isaiah 53 that Philip used to 'preach Jesus' to the Ethiopian pilgrim (8:32–35). But he has already shown us Peter preaching that 'all the prophets' bear witness to this (3:18), and this is the heart of the teaching of the risen Christ (Luke 24:26, 46).

Varied responses

The response is slow but initially positive. Some at least of the Jewish community find Paul's words persuasive (v. 4) and throw in their lot with Paul and Silas, together with a significant number of Greek 'God-fearers', including not a few of the city's leading ladies. But (in what is now becoming a familiar pattern), Paul's message creates as many enemies as friends, and the fault-lines in the community begin to show. 'The Jews' in verse 5 means effectively the rest of the community, all those who were not convinced by Paul's arguments. What binds them together is not jealousy (as in NRSV) but 'zeal', the fundamentalist conviction of righteousness that flies to the defence of a holy God—the same zeal that had driven the young radical Saul to persecute the church.

What follows is Luke's clinical analysis of the makings of a street riot. It's not hard to find troublemakers among the marketplace hangers-on, and once a crowd develops they need to find a scapegoat on which to vent their anger. Luke does not explain who Jason was, although we discover as the story unfolds that he has been acting as host to Paul and his friends (v. 6–7). If he is the same as the person mentioned in Romans 16:21, then he was a relative of Paul.

Turning the world upside down

Did Jason realize what he was letting himself in for? There are times when even a simple act of hospitality becomes a political act. Failing to find Paul at the house, the mob leaders drag Jason and some other believers before the civic authorities. Thessalonica was not a Roman colony but a Greek city, governed by its sovereign *demos*, represented by elected magistrates known locally as *politarchs* (v. 6). The overarching rhetoric of loyalty is the same, however: to maintain even this much-prized degree of autonomy, the Greek cities had to demonstrate their loyalty to the emperor, and nobody wanted to get a name for harbouring political agitators. Precisely what 'decrees of the emperor' were in question here is unclear, but the implication is that Paul's preaching of the crucified Messiah was in effect advocating 'another king' (v. 7) whose lordship challenged Caesar's claims to absolute world authority. It seemed best, therefore, to play safe by extracting surety from Jason, presumably for Paul's good conduct (v. 9).

REFLECTION

Paul and Silas are accused of 'turning the world upside down'
(v. 6). Could that be said of the church today? Should it?

57

From BEROEA *to* ATHENS

Whatever the conditions of Jason's bond, he clearly couldn't undertake to stop Paul preaching the gospel, and presumably didn't want to. So the logical step is to send Paul on his way, a hurried departure by night (v. 10), but in the company of loyal friends who know the way and know, perhaps, that he can expect a better reception when he gets to the next town.

Reception in Beroea

Two cities; two very different faces of the gospel proclamation. Beroea is a kind of reverse image of Thessalonica—same synagogue (v. 10), different reaction to the gospel. Again, Paul goes straight to the Jewish community, and finds a receptive audience, willing and eager to listen to his message and (more importantly) to check it out for themselves, searching the scriptures on a daily basis (v. 11) to see if what Paul says is true. The assumption is that if this message is God speaking, there must be something about it in God's word. Beroea is a model of a responsive community: not just 'some' but 'many' of the Jewish community believe, together with a number of Gentile women of good social standing and quite a few men (v. 12).

Paul has no time to enjoy or consolidate his gains, though. Delegates from Thessalonica turn up and repeat the same rent-a-crowd tactics that had proved so successful there. Having the volatile crowds of the city stirred up (v. 13) is just what these small Jewish communities want above all to avoid: as the situation in Philippi shows (16:20–22), their own position is precarious enough. So their understandable reaction is to get rid of Paul as quickly as possible—although Silas and Timothy, less high-profile and perhaps less inflammatory, remain behind (v. 14). For Paul, it's time to head back to the coast and find a passage to Athens (v. 15).

Waiting in Athens

Paul didn't waste his time in Athens 'just waiting'. This wasn't quite what he had planned, but it was an opportunity to use his eyes and ears to take the measure of this exciting and immensely varied place to which God had brought him. Athens wasn't a bad spot for a bit of enforced leisure! By Paul's time, Greek culture had become inter-national, a near-universal means of communication all over the eastern Mediterranean. Athens, though, remained its emotional heartland, a site immortalized by the poets and dramatists that every Greek-educated child studied at school, and still home to the philosophical schools (like a combination of Oxford, Cambridge and Stratford-upon-Avon). This is the only place in all Paul's journeys where Luke gives us a visual perspective, a tourist's-eye view of the city (v. 16)—but Athens is still described very much through the eyes of a Jewish tourist, someone who sees the city not as a treasure-house of art but as 'full of idols'. It's the beliefs that animate people's lives, not the glories of the past, that interest Paul.

Talking to philosophers

Maybe because of Athens' iconic status, we see a change of tactics here. Paul continues to dialogue with Jewish residents and God-fearers in the synagogue (v. 17), but for the first time he is also prepared to join the more relaxed discussion in the marketplace, a long-standing Athenian tradition going back to the days of Socrates. In this city, the philo-sophers were still part of public life: the Stoics and Epicureans were the most popular exponents of philosophy in the Roman world, not so much cosmologists as lifestyle gurus. But the shadow of Socrates still haunts even this bastion of free speech. Socrates was executed by the good citizens of Athens in 399BC for introducing 'new deities' (*kaina damonia*) that the city did not believe in. The echo would not be lost on Luke's readers when Paul, in this same city, is charged with intro-ducing 'strange deities' (v. 18, *xena daimonia*) and is summoned to explain himself in the ancient assemblage point of the Areopagus (Mars Hill), the place where philosophers were tried (v. 22). There is more than a hint of menace in the polite invitation (vv. 18–20).

REFLECTION

'Active waiting means to be present fully to the moment, in the conviction that something is happening where you are and that you want to be present to it. A waiting person is someone who is present to the moment, who believes that this moment is the moment.'

Nouwen, 1989, p. 103

The UNKNOWN GOD

It's a breathtaking invitation, when you think of it. 'Can we know what you're talking about?' (17:19): literally, 'Is it possible for us to understand this? Can you explain it in words that make sense to us? Or is it just for insiders, the religious people who already talk your language?'

Building bridges

There is a maturity and breadth of vision in Paul's Areopagus speech that is light years away from the stammering, panic-stricken sentences of 14:15–17. In Lystra, Paul was reacting to an immediate situation—taken by surprise, not expecting outsiders to be interested in his message. Here, he has had time to reflect, to listen and observe, and to look more deeply at his audience. He can stand on the outside of the culture and denounce it as 'full of idols' (17:16), or he can look at the people and realize that the city is full of seekers (v. 22), full of people made by God, loved by God, and reaching out to find God (vv. 24–27). Other ancient Greek writers speak of an Athenian custom of dedicating altars to 'unknown gods' (v. 23), but Paul's chance observation is more than just a clever pretext for a sermon. It shows an evangelist prepared to take seriously the reality of the human quest for God. Worship in ignorance (v. 24) is still worship: it deserves respect, not ridicule.

The God beyond

So where do we begin? Accepting the reality of our audience's conceptions doesn't mean being bound by their limitations. Paul has to start by expanding his listeners' view of God. 'I'm not talking about just any old unknown god,' Paul says: 'I'm talking about the God behind the gods, the Creator of the universe' (v. 24). This is the God none of us can claim to 'know', because God is beyond human conception, beyond the most beautiful visual images and temples, beyond the most venerable sacrificial traditions, beyond religion itself (vv. 24–25). This God does not belong to any particular nation or culture. Nations and cultures are part of the world God made (v. 26), so God can't be owned by any one of them. The real God is far above the religious and ethnic divisions of the human race, beyond the furthest reaches of the human imagination (v. 27).

The God beside

Yet this God is also unimaginably close, closer than breathing, closer than family (v. 28). The quotation in verse 28 is from the great evocation of the universal deity of Zeus by the Stoic poet Aratus. And with closeness comes responsibility: this is a God who is not content to be passively sought by humanity, who seeks to evoke a response, who cares enough to nudge us out of our woefully inadequate ways of conceiving God (v. 29). The coming of the Christ means the dawn of a new era, not just for the Jewish people but for the whole of humanity. For both, though, this is a critical moment, a moment of judgment (v. 31, *krisis*; compare John 3:19–21). For the Gentile world, it means that the time of blissful ignorance is past (v. 30). The unknown God wants to be known, and that—for all humanity—involves repentance, a change of heart, being faced with the inescapable demands of a God who cannot be contained in the structures of human religion but only in the person of the risen Lord (v. 31).

We will hear you again

That, for this occasion, is as far as Paul gets. When it comes to the idea of a human being rising from the dead, the philosophers of the Areopagus are frankly incredulous (v. 32), although one or two are convinced (v. 34). As long as Paul stays on the level of philosophical generalities, he's safe; it's the person of Christ that's the stumbling-block. So this great set-piece speech falls short of setting out precisely how the Jewish Messiah is also good news for the Gentile world. It is noticeable, however, how closely the agenda of this speech follows the gospel that Paul himself claims to have preached to the Gentile converts of Thessalonica: see 1 Thessalonians 1:9, and compare the theme of judgment that dominates 1 Thessalonians, a letter written from or very soon after a visit to Athens, according to 1 Thessalonians 3:1.

REFLECTION

'The mission and evangelism of the Church would be much more effective if we were better able to build upon that instinct for God… which is so widely dispersed in our society.'

Peter Forster, Bishop of Chester, 2003

59

TENTMAKING *in* CORINTH

A change of venue, a change of pace, and a chance to settle down for a while after the hustle and hurly-burly of Macedonia and Athens. Corinth was one of the great cities of the ancient world, a cosmopolitan Roman colony and a busy commercial centre straddling the Isthmus. Its twin ports, Cenchreae and Lechaeum, commanded the shipping routes of the Aegean and the Adriatic, and the Diolkos or Portway across the Isthmus created a valuable short cut between eastern and western Mediterranean.

Tentmaking

Here for the first time we get a glimpse of Paul's long-term missionary strategy. The (chance?) meeting with Aquila and Priscilla (v. 2) gives him a more secure base, an opportunity to earn his keep and an entrée into the city's commercial life. The life of a travelling artisan (v. 3) in many ways provided an ideal vehicle for the travelling evangelist. Such artisans were mobile (the tools of the trade could be easily packed up), and had their own networks of business contacts across the Mediterranean. Paul's own ability to deploy a complex network of co-workers may well owe something to his business experience. Travelling artisans had a recognized place in the life of the city, without the special privileges of citizens but accepted (and taxed) as resident aliens. The workshop of Aquila and Priscilla provides a long-term base for Paul's operations, and solves the problem he had experienced in Philippi, Thessalonica and Athens. No one could just turn up in a Greek city (especially if it's also a Roman colony) and start preaching, but the shopfront of a typical workshop, opening directly on to the marketplace, could provide an ideal location for engaging in conversation with passers-by. The shop also gave Paul financial independence, something that was to prove useful in later years in his somewhat stormy relationship with his Corinthian hosts (see 1 Corinthians 9:6).

Aquila and Priscilla

Did Paul already know Aquila and Priscilla? It's not clear from Luke's narrative, but they were to become two of his most trusted associates

(Acts 18:18, 26; 1 Corinthians 16:19; Romans 16:3; 2 Timothy 4:19). The name *skenopoios* (v. 3) is usually translated 'tentmaker', but could be used more widely of leather-workers. Tents, shop awnings, ships' sails or booths for the biennial Isthmian Games could all have provided good trade opportunities in Corinth.

Claudius' edict expelling the Jews from Rome (v. 2) should give us a date for this episode, but things are never as simple as they seem. The Roman writer Suetonius, writing in the early second century AD, mentions in his biography of the emperor Claudius that Claudius 'expelled the [or, some] Jews from Rome, because they were constantly causing disturbances at the instigation of Chrestus' (Suetonius, *Life of Claudius* 25). This could be a garbled reference to riots within the Jewish community in Rome caused by the preaching of Jesus as Messiah (*Christos* would sound the same as *Chrestos* in first-century Greek). If so, this would be the earliest known reference to Christian activity in Rome, and would increase the possibility that Aquila and Priscilla were already Christians when they came to Corinth. A much later historian, Orosius, dates this event to the ninth year of Claudius' reign, AD49, which would fit well with the date of Gallio (see next section) and with other data of New Testament chronology. But this apparently insignificant detail also sounds a warning note: Rome is becoming an ominous presence in the wings of Paul's Aegean journey.

FOR DISCUSSION AND PRAYER

'If this world really is what the church has always said it is, the place and the vehicle of God's activity, and if therefore the world's activity displays all of the signs by which we have learned to recognize God (disfigured but never destroyed by the dirty marks which we make), then our ministry "out there" becomes much clearer… We are to proclaim the word which was before the church began and which is in all the work of the world… Repentance and forgiveness, being God's properties, are also properties of all well run carpenters' shops.'

Ranken, 1997, p. 281

60

CHURCH-PLANTING *in* CORINTH

The workshop in the marketplace provides a fruitful base for church-planting. Corinth was to prove one of Paul's most vibrant and challenging foundations, a church that gave him more heartache than all the others put together—or so it would appear from the letters he wrote to the Corinthians. But little of that appears here. Luke takes us back to the very foundations of the church.

To the Jew first

The initial pattern of evangelization is familiar from Pisidian Antioch (ch. 13) and Thessalonica (ch. 17). Paul begins by getting involved with the local Jewish community and its weekly worship, engaging in dialogue with Jews and with Gentile sympathizers (v. 4). When Silas and Timothy arrive from Macedonia, they find Paul already fully engrossed in the business of the word, busy testifying to the Jews that the Christ, the life-changing and world-changing Messiah of Jewish expectation, is Jesus (v. 5). Once again, though, he fails to persuade the whole community (v. 6). The action of shaking out the garments is a prophetic action that indicates absolution from a spiritual responsibility (see 13:51). Like Ezekiel (Ezekiel 3:18–20), Paul is acutely conscious of his prophetic responsibility to proclaim God's word to his own people (compare 1 Corinthians 9:16–23). Only after he is convinced that the Jewish community has rejected his message does he feel free to turn to the Gentiles.

It is important not to confuse Paul's words in verse 6 with the so-called 'blood libel' of Matthew 27:25. This is not about assigning responsibility for the death of Jesus (neither Luke nor Paul ever implies that all Jews everywhere bear that responsibility) but about the individual hearers accepting responsibility for their own response to the Christ. If prophets fail to preach the word assigned to them, then they must bear the heavy responsibility of failing to warn those to whom they are sent. But if they have delivered their message faithfully, then the responsibility for accepting or rejecting it lies with the listener. Even so, Paul's decision to go to the Gentiles is not a decision for all time but a decision for Corinth: the drama of 'to the Jew first' will continue to be played out in each place he visits (see 18:19).

And also to the Greek

Once again, the preaching of Jesus as the Christ provokes a crisis, a double effect of rejection and acceptance. The move from Jew to Greek is described with some ceremony as a physical move from one building to another (vv. 6–7: 'synagogue' here must mean a building, since Luke speaks of it as 'adjoining' the house of Titius Justus). There is a sense here of a real community, probably known both to the author and to his first readers. Titius Justus (v. 7) is not mentioned anywhere else in the New Testament, but Crispus (v. 8) is named in 1 Corinthians 1:14 as someone baptized by Paul. Both names are Latin, reflecting Corinth's close links with Rome as a colonial foundation. As a synagogue official, Crispus would have been a wealthy patron of good standing in the city, a significant loss to the synagogue and a catch for Paul's splinter group. Titius Justus, too, as a house owner, would have been a valuable acquisition with the facilities to act as host to the church (which may be why Luke mentions him and Crispus).

I am with you

However (as John Wesley used to say), 'the best of all is, God is with us': whatever qualms Paul may have felt at leaving the Jewish community, a dream gives him the assurance of God's presence (vv. 9–10). The message is not only 'I will be with you' as you step into an uncertain future, but 'I am already here'. Like Peter in Caesarea (ch. 10), Paul finds that God is already at work in this confusing pagan city: there is no territory outside the purview of the living God. So there's a sense of relief about the verb 'stayed' (NRSV) in verse 11. Eighteen months is longer than Paul has stayed anywhere for some time, and it enables him to do real foundational work in Corinth, teaching the word and building up the church. This is bread-and-butter stuff that Luke assumes but does not tell us about, except in this summary form.

REFLECTION

'Dialogue' and 'testimony' are two of the key words in
Luke's description of Paul's church-planting. How important
are they to us today?

61

ACTS 18:12–22

LEAVING CORINTH

This period of settled expansion was not to last. Paul, in Luke's narrative, is not destined to settle anywhere for more than a couple of years. We are coming to the final stages of the drama, with the looming presence of the imperial city beginning to exert its pull over Paul's journey.

The new governor

Corinth was the administrative capital of the Roman province of Achaea, and the seat of the proconsul. The arrival of a new governor from Rome for his one-year tour of duty provides an opportunity for Paul's opponents in the synagogue to try to get rid of him (v. 12). Gallio was the brother of the philosopher Seneca, and by chance we can actually date the year of his proconsulship from an inscription discovered at Delphi, which fixes his appointment to the twelfth year of Claudius' reign: AD51/52. The confrontation with Gallio serves as a foretaste of Paul's coming confrontation with the power of imperial Rome, and brings the apostle face to face with the representative of the emperor who had just expelled the Jews from Rome.

Before the tribunal

Paul has left a trail of civic disturbance behind him on his unruly progression through Macedonia, and damaging charges have been laid at his door: teaching un-Roman customs (16:21), acting against the emperor's decrees, and advocating another king (17:7). These serious political accusations are so far unanswered, and the confrontation with Gallio gives Luke an opportunity to quote a ruling that Paul's teaching, however troublesome it may be for the Jewish community, is not in contravention to Roman law. The Roman empire was not a totalitarian state in the modern sense, and Rome had neither the desire nor the means to regulate the empire's myriad ways of worshipping God. The only 'law' that has been infringed by Paul's teaching, Gallio declares, is the law of the Jewish community—and that is purely an internal affair (vv. 14–15). Gallio's ruling thus identifies Paul's messianic Judaism as a legitimate sect within the broad spectrum of first-century Judaism, and establishes the important point that this Roman official at least sees no legal or moral fault in the activities of the church.

Luke does not tell us who Sosthenes is (v. 17), but if he is the same person as Paul's co-writer in 1 Corinthians 1:1, this is another synagogue official who has gone over to Paul's party.

Moving on

Despite his vindication at the tribunal, Paul takes this fresh outbreak of hostility as the signal to depart. It is more than three years since he left Antioch and he clearly feels that it is time to touch base again, so, after taking some time to tidy up his affairs, he takes ship for Syria (v. 18).

The visit to the barber's in Cenchreae is a tantalizing note. Paul's vow should probably be understood in light of the nazirite vows of the Old Testament (see Numbers 6:2, 9), where the shaving of the head is one of the marks of a life dedicated to God's service, and it may be linked with Paul's planned return to the Jewish heartlands. He is not leaving alone, however, and does not make directly for Syria. Aquila and Priscilla (perhaps reflecting on their earlier experience of being hounded out of Rome as Jews) decide to move on too. This may be the point at which they became Paul's active co-workers in his ongoing mission, but they had no business in Syria, and Ephesus seemed as good a place as any to set up shop again—both in business and (as we shall see) in the gospel. Paul is not yet ready to settle down in Asia. He can't resist testing the waters, however, with a visit to the synagogue (v. 19), and finds a favourable response (v. 20), enough to make him promise to return (v. 21).

Touching base

So, finally (and much more quietly than on his return at the end of the first mission in 14:26–28), Paul slips back home to Antioch via Caesarea and Jerusalem. (The unexplained 'going up' in verse 22 probably indicates a visit to Jerusalem, perhaps to fulfil the vow undertaken in Cenchreae.) Paul's mission 'is not only preaching the gospel, converting people, and founding churches, but also creating and strengthening the ties among Christians and between churches' (Gonzalez 2001, p. 213).

REFLECTION

'In the biblical vision, to believe in Jesus Christ implies and requires joining the community of the faithful… To believe in Jesus Christ is indeed a very personal matter, but not a private one.'

Gonzalez 2001, p. 214

62

APOLLOS & PAUL

Luke's story in the second half of Acts is very much focused on Paul, but the next two episodes serve as a salutary reminder of the variety and diversity of early Christianity, and of the many criss-crossing storylines that Luke can only hint at.

Travelling up-country

Paul himself spends some time in Antioch (v. 23), perhaps waiting for the travelling season to open up the high passes of the Taurus again. Then it's back up through the Cilician Gates to make a systematic visitation of the disciples in 'the region of Galatia and Phrygia'. This is a variant of the phrase in 16:6 but probably means exactly the same—that is, the churches in Derbe, Iconium, Lystra and Pisidian Antioch founded by Paul and Barnabas on the first journey. Thus begins what is often referred to as Paul's 'Third Missionary Journey', although, as we can see, Luke does not mark it as a significant new beginning in comparison with the first (13:1–3) and second (15:36—16:10) journeys. It's more helpful to think of it as 'Phase 3' of the Pauline mission, which takes us down to Acts 20:38. This is the period of Paul's most intense letter-writing activity (1 and 2 Corinthians were written from Ephesus), the period when Paul describes himself as consumed by the daily pressure of 'the care of all the churches' (2 Corinthians 11:28). Luke never mentions Paul's letters (one of the many minor puzzles in his portrait of Paul), but on this trip we see Paul engaged as much in consolidation and encouragement as in mission, busily trying to keep in touch with an ever-expanding network of churches.

Apollos

In Ephesus, however, things have been moving on in Paul's absence: the church in Luke's story is never dependent on its 'stars' to make progress. Aquila and Priscilla, while still attending the synagogue (v. 26), are part of a circle of 'brothers' (v. 27): compare 1 Corinthians 16:19, where Paul sends greetings to Corinth from the church in their house.

Meanwhile, a new voice arrives from a totally unexpected quarter.

Apollos was a Jew from Alexandria (v. 24), a member of the largest and most prosperous Jewish community in the Mediterranean diaspora. Alexandria was a sophisticated university city (home to the famous Museum and Library founded by the Ptolemies), and a major forum for interchange of Greek and Jewish culture at the highest level. Apollos was, Luke tells us, an eloquent man: good with words, highly educated and sophisticated, a man with all the verbal dexterity that impressed the Greek world (which Paul, by his own account, lacked: see 1 Corinthians 2:1–5). But Apollos was no mere academic or flashy speaker. He was also learned in the scriptures, able to combine the best of Jewish and Greek culture. More surprisingly, he was also 'instructed in the way of the Lord', and is able to draw on a fund of stories and teaching about Jesus, although he 'knows only the baptism of John' (v. 25).

Collaborative ministry

Had Apollos visited Judea and encountered John the Baptist's preaching there? We shall never know, but we have no warrant for doubting that Apollos was a genuine believer, even though there was something missing in his teaching, which Priscilla and Aquila notice when they hear him in the synagogue. Rather than issuing a public corrective (which would be humiliating) or telling him that he is not qualified to teach at all (which would be discouraging), Priscilla and her husband take him aside privately to share their own understanding of the Way (v. 26)—a brave step, considering the differing educational and social levels of the tentmakers and the scholar from Alexandria. The tiny group of brothers in Ephesus welcomes the newcomer with generosity, recognizing his gifts and encouraging him to use them in the Lord's service and follow his own vision of mission to Corinth (vv. 27–28). Apollos then disappears from Luke's story, although Paul mentions him in 1 Corinthians 16:12 as a trusted colleague who had built on the foundation that Paul laid in Corinth (1 Corinthians 3:4–22). If Apollos' Corinthian fan club were inclined to set him up as a rival to Paul (1 Corinthians 1:12), Paul is careful not to blame Apollos himself.

FOR DISCUSSION AND PRAYER
How quick are we to welcome God's gifts in others?

63

ACTS 19:1–12

PAUL *in* EPHESUS

Paul, meanwhile, has been working his way down towards Ephesus by the upland route (v. 1), coming overland from Phrygia. This is the same journey he had attempted to make at 16:6—and this time there is no impediment. Ephesus presents a new challenge to Paul. The challenge of the unknown always appealed to Paul's adventurous instincts. Ephesus is different, though: Paul is not the first to preach the gospel there, and he has to work out how to follow his own vision and vocation while respecting the vision that God has given to others. Ephesus raises the question: when our vision differs from somebody else's, how do we know what is right? What makes discipleship *Christian*?

The baptism of John

We already know that there is a small fellowship group in Ephesus, working with Aquila and Priscilla (18:26–27). It is more of a surprise to encounter another group of disciples who have links with John the Baptist (v. 3). Quite how the Baptist's message reached Ephesus is not clear, but it is important to remember that there were many trading and community links between Palestine and the major cities of the diaspora, and similar groups such as the Qumran sect had adherents in a variety of city locations. Are these people Christians? Luke doesn't attempt to define them except as 'disciples' (v. 1), which in Acts normally means disciples of Jesus (9:26; 11:29; 13:52). The key question for Paul is, 'Did you receive the Holy Spirit when you came to faith?' (v. 2) and the answer sheds light on the deficiencies of John's baptism. It is a baptism that looks backwards, a genuine movement of the soul leading to repentance (v. 4). It expresses a repugnance for everything in our lives that separates from God, and it's an essential part of the divine plan in preparing a people cleansed from sin (see Luke 1:17, 76).

The gift of the Spirit

Looking back, though, is not enough. The message of the gospel is about looking forward to the one who is coming, that is, Jesus (v. 4). And baptism in the name of Jesus (v. 5) means baptism not just in water but also in the Holy Spirit (Luke 3:16). Christian baptism comes with a promise attached: it's not just about lamenting our sins and letting go

146

of the past, but also about accepting the invitation into God's future, into a community empowered by God's indwelling Spirit. Sometimes, as here, that indwelling is manifested visibly and audibly through identifiable charismatic gifts like speaking in tongues and prophesying (v. 6), but Paul's letters make it clear that that is only half the story. All Christians are promised the gift of the Spirit, as God's life-giving, transforming initiative for changing lives from the inside (see Acts 2:38–39; Romans 12:1–2; Galatians 5:16–23). There are many baptized Christians today who have 'not even heard that there is a Holy Spirit' (v. 2)—or, at least, don't realize that the Holy Spirit is for them.

Peter and Paul

Several aspects of this story remind us of Peter's role earlier in Acts. Like Peter, Paul has the power to release the gift of the Holy Spirit through the laying on of hands (v. 6; compare 8:17). Like Peter, Paul performs extraordinary miracles, so much so that spiritual power even leaks out from his person at one remove (vv. 11–12, compare 5:15), although Luke is careful to stress that the source of this power is not Paul but God. And, as with Peter, the net result is a whole population awestruck with 'fear'—that is, the proper response to the numinous presence of God (compare v. 17 with 5:12–14).

Yet Paul's mission is not primarily about impressing the crowds with a demonstration of spiritual power. His bread-and-butter of mission is the careful, patient, person-to-person work of dialogue and persuasion (v. 8), working within existing community structures for three months before deciding to make a break (v. 9). Unusually, here in Ephesus Paul moves from the synagogue not into a house but into a school. The school of Tyrannus (v. 10) was probably a private building used for lectures during the morning but available for hire when it was not in use for regular classes. It's a reminder of the continuing importance of 'going public' with the gospel, communicating the good news not just inside the church but in a place—and in a language—that is accessible to all.

PRAYER

Father, confirm and strengthen in us the promise of our baptism, that we may daily increase in your Holy Spirit more and more, until we come to your everlasting kingdom: through your Son, our Saviour Jesus Christ.

MAGIC & MIRACLE

Right from the beginning of the Gospel, Jesus and his followers have had to answer the persistent charge that the spiritual power seen at work in them is not heavenly but demonic (compare Mark 3:20–30). Paul's active missionary career began with a confrontation with a magician (13:6–12), and it ends with a scene that makes clear the radical difference between magic and miracle. Luke wants to make quite sure that his readers won't confuse the two.

The sons of Sceva

Luke's account of Paul's extraordinary charismatic power (19:12) highlights the ever-present danger, for those to whom God entrusts such power, of worship becoming attached to the individual's name and not to the true source of all spiritual power. When spiritual power becomes a commodity that can be carried by inanimate objects, we are in dangerous waters. The cult of saints and their relics has always been a part of Christian history. It's a testimony to the spiritual reality located in certain individuals, but (as all the saints are aware) that reality always has to be referred back to the God who gives the gift. Quite who the 'sons of Sceva' were (v. 14) is not clear: the 'high priest' himself could not have operated in Ephesus, but (as we have seen) Ephesus had a large and vigorous Jewish community with many links with Jerusalem, and Jews had a name in the ancient world as powerful healers and magicians. We know from the ancient magical papyri that such magicians operated all over the ancient Mediterranean, drawing cheerfully and indiscriminately on any name that held the promise of power—pagan, Jewish or Christian.

Who are you?

The underlying message of Luke's story is clear: don't mess about with spiritual powers, good or bad (v. 16). There are real spiritual forces at work here, and no parrot-fashion recitation of magic formulae will control them: 'Jesus I know, and Paul I know; but who are you?' (v. 15). The power Paul wielded was real, but it was bought at deep personal cost, and sprang out of an encounter with the self-giving love through which Jesus won the ultimate victory over evil on the cross (see 2 Corinthians 12:1–10; Galatians 6:14–17). On the field of spiritual conflict, short cuts are dangerous. It is never a matter of simply finding the right words to say. The spirit 'knows' Paul—recognizes his name as one that has currency in the spiritual realm—Luke implies, because Paul's own identity is defined by his relationship with the Lord Jesus, 'whose I am, and whom I serve' (19:17; 27:23).

There is no room for second-hand faith here (v. 13). Knowing Jesus as Lord provides the only safe answer to the question, 'Who are you?' The true path to spiritual integrity, or spiritual power, may lead through gifted individuals to whom God has given exceptional gifts of leadership or teaching or healing, but the ultimate question of spiritual identity can only be answered by each of us alone, face to face with the unknown God.

Bonfire of books

The experience of the exorcists carries a sharp warning for anyone inclined to use the name of Jesus as a short cut to spiritual power. Ephesus had a name in the ancient world as a centre for the production of magic books, and there must have been a number of believers who saw the name of Jesus as a useful addition to a successful spiritual portfolio. But Jesus can never be just one name among others. Christian discipleship means making choices, and in this passage we see the dawning realization (it doesn't happen all at once!) that these magic practices were incompatible with their newfound faith. Hence the slow process of inner acknowledgment (we have to admit these things to ourselves first), followed by public confession (v. 18), and then the very necessary renunciation of the visible and material (not to say expensive) expressions of that other life (v. 19). Faith is not only about initial commitment. It's also about the slow and painfully honest process of discovering what the Lordship of Christ really means. But when believers are prepared to do that—and do it publicly—then the power of God's word becomes visible to all the world (v. 20).

REFLECTION

'The demon sees that it knows Jesus. Why? Because Jesus faced evil, entered its dwellings, walked with the sick, the lame, and the sinners, was criticized, insulted, and eventually killed by the powers of evil, and through all this he came out victorious.'

Gonzalez 2001, p. 227

65

BEING CHURCH *in* EPHESUS

This chapter brings together in a vivid and dramatic way many of the different perceptions of what it means to be church in the urban world of the first century. To insiders, it means being part of a dynamic and diverse network of autonomous house churches. This is the world we glimpse in Paul's letters. But Acts also shows what the church looks like to outsiders: Jewish splinter group, philosophical school, wonder-working cult. Here it's beginning to look alarmingly like a rival to the powerful local trade guilds, and it is this confrontation that forms the climax to Paul's stay in Ephesus.

God's plans and ours

We are beginning to move into the final phase of Paul's story. It's a story that will end with Paul's arrival in Rome as a prisoner (ch. 28), but Paul doesn't know that yet, and what we see in chapters 19—21 is Paul's gradual realization of the new direction in which God is calling him—and of what it will cost. The first stirrings are here, in the bustle of making plans and getting ready to move on.

Paul's stay in Ephesus (more than two years, 19:10) is the longest stay that Luke records anywhere, and we know it as one of the most fruitful periods of Paul's letter-writing activity. Acts doesn't mention the letters, or the conflicts in Corinth that occupied so much of Paul's attention in Ephesus. Even more mysteriously, Luke doesn't mention the 'collection for the saints' that motivated Paul's final trip to Macedonia and Achaea (see 2 Corinthians 8—9). Perhaps, writing with hindsight, he finds it too painful to record this abortive project, which Paul conceived as a way of holding together the Gentile churches and the mother church in Jerusalem, a project about which Paul himself records his hopes and misgivings in Romans 15:25–32.

What he does tell us is that Paul is getting ready to hit the road again (v. 21), preparing a pastoral visitation of the churches founded in the second phase of his mission in Macedonia (Philippi, Thessalonica, Beroea) and Achaea (Corinth, Cenchreae, and perhaps others we don't know about). The plan is to do a round trip across Greece before returning to Jerusalem—not as crazy as it sounds, given that a sea voyage direct from Corinth to Jerusalem would cut out the long overland trek across Asia. Somewhere in there, too (as we see in Romans 15:22–24, which was written from Corinth on the last stage of this round trip), is a conviction that God is calling him to go further west, to Rome itself (v. 21). 'Must' is one of Luke's code-words for what God has planned, although the manner and final destination of Paul's last voyage to the imperial city was to turn out very differently from what the apostle himself envisaged (Romans 15:24).

Demetrius the silversmith

First, though, Ephesus has a final surprise in store—which perhaps makes it clear to Paul that it's high time to leave! As in Thessalonica, Luke sets out the anatomy of this riot very carefully (v. 23). It surfaces as a face-off between Paul's uncompromising preaching of mono-theism ('Real gods are not made with hands', v. 26) and the city's most famous cult, the worship of Diana (Greek Artemis) of the Ephesians. Any good illustrated Bible Dictionary will show you a picture of the famous many-breasted cult image of Artemis, the centre of the civic cult at Ephesus and a major reason for the city's wealth (v. 27). Archaeologists have found silver mini-shrines of the type Luke describes (v. 24), manufactured in their thousands for the tourist/pilgrim trade. But as Luke tells the story, the underlying motive for the disturbance is not religious but commercial: Demetrius and his co-workers are frightened by the prospect of losing their trade (vv. 24–26). This concern is echoed half a century later by Pliny the Younger, the Roman governor of Bithynia in AD111, who complains that the success of Christianity is having a negative impact on the sales of sacrificial animals at all the local shrines (Pliny, *Letters* 10.96).

To any pagan reading Luke's story, the message is clear: the preach-ing of God's word is making serious inroads into one of the major cult centres of the eastern Mediterranean. To Jewish readers, it sends an equally clear message: Paul is faithfully proclaiming the worship of the living God.

REFLECTION

If the preaching of the gospel is having any real effect,
sooner or later it will start to touch the political and economic
structures with which our lives are entwined—and then,
watch out for fireworks!

DIANA *of the* EPHESIANS

Demetrius succeeds in whipping up a full-scale religious demonstration, which erupts into the theatre, one of the biggest public spaces in the city (vv. 28–29). Two of Paul's travelling companions are caught up in the excitement—Gaius and Aristarchus from Macedonia. This is the first time Luke has mentioned these delegates from the Macedonian churches, who have become part of Paul's mobile team. We discover later that Aristarchus comes from Thessalonica (20:4), and is probably the same person who accompanies Paul on his final voyage to Rome (27:2) and later sends greetings as a companion of Paul from prison (Philemon 24; Colossians 4:10). Gaius was a common Roman forename, and there are at least three of Paul's associates called Gaius, one from Corinth (Romans 16:23; 1 Corinthians 1:14), one from Derbe (Acts 20:4) and this one from Macedonia.

The wild-beast show

Paul sees this as a golden opportunity to address the whole civic body in the theatre (v. 30), but his friends know better. Ephesians are not philosophers, and this is no Areopagus. Passions are running high (v. 32): think of a cross between a football crowd and a political rally. The 'officials' (v. 31, NRSV, literally 'Asiarchs') were responsible for the maintenance of the emperor-cult for the whole of Asia. Ephesus was the provincial centre for this politically sensitive cult, and although there was no formal conflict between the imperial and civic cults, it may be that the Asiarchs too were keeping a wary watch on this violent display of public attachment to the city's more traditional cult.

Silent witness

Unusually, Paul has hardly a word to say in this episode, yet it highlights the courage and endurance needed to witness to the one God in a pagan city. The whole scene speaks volumes about the delicate positioning of 'the Way' in the religious maelstrom of the great cities of the eastern empire. Historians have argued in the past that Christianity made an impact because people were becoming disillusioned with the old gods —but this is simply not true. In Ephesus, civic pride and identity were integrally bound up with the cult of 'the great Artemis' (v. 34), believed locally to have chosen the city as her official 'temple keeper'. The ancient cult-image was believed to have fallen from heaven (v. 35), and was probably a meteorite. Jews in these pagan cities maintained a precarious position.

It is not clear whether Alexander (v. 33) was put up to speak by people in the crowd, by Paul's friends, or by members of the Jewish community, anxious to distance themselves from Paul and his message. In any case, he gets no chance to speak (v. 34). Jews were normally accepted members of the city's polyglot commercial community, but in this highly charged atmosphere no one who looked like an outsider was going to get a hearing.

Political pressures

This story also subtly distances Paul and his message from the rioting crowd. It reveals the overwhelming concern of the city authorities to maintain law and order. The 'town clerk' (v. 35) has only one thing in mind—to dissolve this illegal assembly and peacefully disperse the chanting crowd. In his eagerness to keep the peace, the town clerk unwittingly makes a very important statement in Paul's defence: he is not a 'temple-robber' and has not directly blasphemed the city's patron goddess (v. 37). Both Jews and Christians were often charged with being 'atheists' and bad-mouthing other people's religious beliefs, but Luke is keen to show that this is no way to bring people to belief in the one God. And, finally, Luke's story chillingly reveals the hidden pressure exerted by Rome on the Greek cities. Anything that might attract the censure of the governor (and riots and illegal assemblies certainly would, v. 40) has to be suppressed or channelled into a more legal format (v. 39). Rome encouraged the cities to keep up the forms of local self-government, and provided an outlet for litigation through the local assizes run by the Roman proconsul on his annual tour of duty in this province (v. 38). The implication for Luke's readers (who should remember what happened last time Paul was brought before a proconsul, in 18:12–17) is that, in a legal court, no charges against his message would stand.

PRAYER

Lord, teach us to approach other people's beliefs with respect,
and to witness with courage to you, the living God.

67

ACT FOUR: PAUL *the* PRISONER

So the final stage of Luke's drama begins. Ephesus (although Paul does not know it) marks the end of an era of church-planting and missionary preaching, and the beginning of Paul's transformation from missionary to prisoner. The Greek word for witness (*martus*) also gives us our word 'martyr', and this is the point at which Paul begins to understand that being a witness is not only about talking but also about being prepared to lay your life on the line.

To Troas via Corinth

The story begins innocuously enough, with the long-planned trip to revisit the churches of Macedonia and Achaea (v. 1; see 19:21). It is intended as a trip of encouragement and consolidation (v. 2), but Paul's reappearance triggers a sharp counter-reaction in the Jewish community (presumably in Corinth), and the original plan to take ship from Corinth to Jerusalem is abandoned (v. 3). Instead, the whole group will return via the overland route, up the coast to Thessalonica and then across to the coast of Asia Minor.

The party is looking more and more like a formal delegation (v. 4), with representatives from three of the areas in which Paul has worked: Macedonia, Galatia and Asia. Sopater may be the same person as the Sosipater of Romans 16:21. Tychicus turns up again in the later Pauline letters (see Colossians 4:7; Ephesians 6:21; Titus 3:12; 2 Timothy 4:12); Trophimus must be the Gentile mentioned in Acts 21:29. Intriguingly, there is no delegate from Achaea, but we must not forget the old friend who now rejoins the party, as the 'we-narrative' resumes in Philippi, just where we left our mysterious companion on the second phase of Paul's mission (v. 6; see 16:16).

Before there was a Sunday

The Asian members of the party may well have gone straight to Troas to wait for Paul there (v. 5). Paul himself lingers in Philippi to celebrate the feast of Passover with his friends (v. 6), then crosses over to Troas to spend a week with the community there. As a starting point for a fateful trip to Rome, Troas would have had interesting resonances for Roman readers. Ancient Troy was the ruined city from which Aeneas set out, in Virgil's great epic poem *The Aeneid*, for a voyage of tragedy and shipwreck that culminated in the founding of the city of Rome. But instead of epic grandeur, Luke gives us a vivid vignette of the worshipping life of these first Christians. Before there was such a thing as Sunday, Christians had to squeeze their meetings into whatever time was available, even if it meant staying up all night on the first day of the week before going off for a day's work or travel (v. 7). So, just as Pliny, the Roman governor of next-door Bithynia in AD111, tells of Christians meeting 'before dawn' to sing hymns to Christ (Pliny, *Letters* 10.96), Luke gives us this charming domestic scene of the night-time meeting in the third-storey room of a tenement building (v. 9), lit by smoky lamps (v. 8).

Unlucky Eutychus

The meeting is for the breaking of bread (v. 7) in memory of Jesus' last Passover meal with his disciples, but Paul also has a lot to say to this precious little group whom he may never see again. That's one reason why unlucky Eutychus falls asleep (v. 9). His name (which means 'Lucky') is often a slave-name, and he may already have had a long day's work, but the fumes from the lamps could also have had a soporific effect. It's not clear from Luke's story whether the fall left him dead or merely unconscious, but either way Paul's prompt action (which recalls the prophet Elijah in 1 Kings 17:17–24) saves the boy's life (vv. 10, 12). Like the widow of Zarephath, Luke's readers will recognize the life-giving power at work in this man of God. It's entirely appropriate that the episode closes with Paul 'breaking the bread' with this tiny group of disciples (v. 11), in the memorial meal with which Christians down the ages have gathered on the first day of the week to celebrate the victory of life over death.

PRAYER

*'Thanks be to God, who gives us the victory
through our Lord Jesus Christ.'*

1 Corinthians 15:57

68

FAREWELL *at* MILETUS

The narrative becomes a ceremonial progression down the west coast of Asia Minor (vv. 13–16), listing the islands and ports of call on a typical island-hopping Aegean coastal voyage. Paradoxically, this creates a sense of suspense as we move slowly down the coast, stopping to pick up Paul in Assos, since for some unexplained reason he had decided to do the first part of the journey on foot (v. 13). We come to share Paul's sense of frustration at the slowness of the voyage (v. 16); after celebrating Passover in Philippi, he is anxious to get to Jerusalem within 50 days in time for Pentecost—and we've already spent a week in Troas (20:6). But coastal traders follow their own timetables, and a few days' enforced delay at Miletus gives Paul the opportunity to summon the leaders of the Ephesian house churches for a farewell discourse.

The elders from Ephesus

It is only a few months since Paul left Ephesus (20:3), but we seem to have shifted into a different time-frame altogether. The 'elders' of the church (v. 17) were never mentioned in chapter 19, but we should not forget that Paul was not involved in setting up the church in Ephesus. It was already well established before he got there, and we can reasonably infer that Priscilla and Aquila would have followed the same pattern of church structures that Paul had instituted in 14:23. Diaspora synagogues normally had a governing body of local 'elders', and the early church seems to have followed this pattern. It's a timely reminder that while Paul was acting as a kind of evangelistic front-man in his public lectures in the school of Tyrannus (19:9–10), the day-to-day work of the local church was going on behind the scenes.

Paul the pastor

Now, however, in this long valedictory speech, Luke gives us a rare insight into Paul's pastoral concerns for the leaders of the local church. He has told us often enough of Paul's continued determination to build up and encourage the churches he founded (14:22; 15:32; 20:2). Now we get a chance to eavesdrop on Paul the pastor in action—not necessarily a real speech, but (as Luke's speeches often are) a paradigmatic composition putting together the kinds of things Paul would have said in so many different places and on so many different occasions. Not surprisingly, this speech is the closest of all Paul's Acts speeches to the sort of thing he says in his letters, which are dealing with the same kinds of issues. But, rather than dealing with particular problems in a church situation, this speech gives a general impression of Paul the pastor as Luke feels he should be remembered.

Looking back

As so often in his letters, Paul begins by looking back over a life dedicated to his Lord's service (vv. 18–21; compare Philippians 1; Galatians 1; 1 Thessalonians 2). It's a life in which there is no hiding place: 'You know how I was with you the whole time' (v. 18). What we are says just as much about the gospel as what we say. As a pastor, Paul had to make his whole life available to the people he worked with as a testimony to the gospel, a life defined not by success but by enslavement to his Lord (v. 19). This is the relationship that defines all others in Paul's life: see Romans 1:1; Philippians 1:1; Galatians 1:10; 2 Corinthians 4:5. The pastor's life has to be a Christ-like life, a life of humility (Philippians 2:3, 8), of tears and trials and persecutions (1 Thessalonians 1:6–7; 2:14–16; Philippians 1:12–17, 27–30). But none of this has deflected Paul from his prime task of announcing and teaching the gospel message of repentance and faith in Jesus, both publicly (in the synagogue, in the school of Tyrannus) and from house to house (vv. 20–21), a good summary of the Pauline mission.

REFLECTION

Do I define my service to Christ in terms of 'my ministry',
or do I define my ministry in terms of service to Christ?

69

I HAVE FINISHED MY COURSE

And now? There's a note of foreboding as Paul describes his present state, still technically a free agent but 'bound in the Spirit' (v. 22)— a chilling glimpse of what lies ahead, even though we have as yet no hint of the events that will lead to Paul's eventual imprisonment. For Paul, the future at this moment is opaque, full of prophetic hints of bonds and persecution in store (v. 23). The powerful metaphor of a race almost finished (v. 24) echoes the prison epistles (compare Philippians 3:14; 2 Timothy 4:7). Yet Paul refuses to let the future's darkness deter him from carrying out the ministry with which he has been entrusted, the marvellous mission of making God's grace known in the world. This is what's in his mind as he writes to Rome from Corinth before setting out for Jerusalem (Romans 15:15–24); and here too he has the conviction, looking back, of having fulfilled the task entrusted to him, of having 'fully proclaimed' the gospel (Romans 15:19). Even if these people never see him again in this life (v. 25), he knows that he has discharged his duty, making full use of every opportunity to pass on every insight into God's purposes (vv. 26–27).

Tend the flock

This leaves the elders, humanly speaking, on their own. They won't be able to rely on Paul's leadership any more. So there's a sober note of warning in verses 28–31: take care, be alert, there are wolves about. You can expect attacks both from outside the community and (perhaps more alarming) from inside. Isn't Paul worried about leaving such an inexperienced local team to carry on in his absence? No, he says, you don't need to worry, because your confidence, like mine, rests not on yourselves but on God. It is God who has put you where you are and given you a ministry to fulfil there, a distinctive ministry entrusted to you directly by God's Holy Spirit (v. 28).

Being 'local' is no more and no less important in the divine economy than having a worldwide itinerant ministry like Paul's. You are *episkopoi*, Paul says—'guardians' or 'overseers'—a term which later meant 'bishop' but here is another name for the local elders (20:17). That means being entrusted with the enormous responsibility and privilege of shepherding the flock which is God's (not yours or mine), a flock that God has acquired at enormous cost. Put simply: if God thought it was worth dying for, you'd better take good care of it! So don't be surprised if you have a few sleepless nights (v. 31). Your ultimate resource, like mine, is the infinite reserves of God's grace, a grace which has the power to build you up and bring you through to the inheritance that God has in store for all his saints (v. 32). The key word here is 'commend', a word that appears again in a different form in 2 Timothy 1:12 to express the double paradox of Christian ministry. It's something that God commits to us, but we can only do it insofar as we commit it (and ourselves) to God.

Remember the little things

'Remember the little things that I taught you,' said the sixth-century Welsh saint David on his deathbed, and Paul too closes with a list of 'little things'. Ultimately, the gospel of grace has to be lived out in real lives. That's what people remember, and that's what apostles are for. Discipleship in the ancient world meant, above all else, watching your teacher's lifestyle like a hawk so as to learn what wisdom really meant, so the most important task of the apostles was to model in their own lives what they had learnt from their own Master.

Like Peter (3:6), Paul has learnt that ministry is not about money-making (v. 33); on the contrary, he has worked with his own hands to support himself during the three years he was in Ephesus (v. 34; 18:1–4). And this pattern of self-support, even though it looks contrary to the apostolic lifestyle authorized by Jesus (compare Paul's discussion in 1 Corinthians 9), can be directly linked with Jesus' teaching on giving (20:35; Paul draws a similar parallel from the self-giving pattern of Jesus' life in 2 Corinthians 8:9). Interestingly, this is a saying of Jesus which is not recorded in the Gospels; it is a salutary reminder that the Gospel writers could only record a fraction of all Jesus' sayings (see John 20:30; 21:25).

REFLECTION AND PRAYER

'I thank my God every time I remember you, constantly praying with joy in every one of my prayers for all of you… confident of this, that the one who began a good work among you will bring it to completion.'

Philippians 1:3–5

70

ACTS 20:36—21:17

TOWARDS JERUSALEM

Contrary to popular belief, Paul wasn't all head and no heart! This passage shows us the deep affection in which he was held, and goes some way to revealing the real person behind his pastoral ministry.

Miletus to Tyre

We don't normally think of Paul as inspiring affection, but the Miletus speech dissolves into an emotional farewell scene (vv. 36–38), which forms a fitting climax to Paul's pastoral ministry. Now the voyage resumes (21:1), with the same loving and leisurely evocation of the passing scene. This is a working ship, probably a coastal trader, but its passengers, after all the emotion of Miletus, have an unexpected period of leisure with nothing to do but watch the unfolding panorama from the ship's deck. Patara means a change of ship, finding a boat heading east to Phoenicia (v. 2); and then, with Cyprus slipping below the horizon on the port side (lots of nautical language here: Luke clearly enjoys sailing), a quiet, unmarked landing in Tyre, where the boat is to discharge her cargo (v. 3).

Tyre to Ptolemais

There is an increasing sense that this voyage is in God's hands. Mysterious, unexplained disciples appear to offer hospitality for a few days in Tyre (v. 4: Luke hasn't told us before that there is a church here). But now the warnings begin again (see 20:23), and we have another affecting seashore farewell (v. 5), with tearful women and children. Then it's back on board (v. 6) as the boat resumes the next stage of her voyage, described in equally loving, lingering detail, before meeting and greeting a new set of brothers in Ptolemais (v. 7). It's fascinating in these last stages of Paul's journey to see how the Way has been spreading like an underground root system in all sorts of unexpected directions. Luke clearly doesn't expect us to conclude that the story he tells is the whole story of the early church (although we often read it that way).

Ptolemais to Caesarea

The next day, it's round the Carmel headland to Caesarea, the main port of debarkation for Jerusalem (v. 8). Here we meet an old friend, Philip the evangelist, one of the 'seven' (6:5; 8:5–40). Philip has four daughters, all prophets (v. 9), although it is not they who provide the conclusive prophecy for Paul. Agabus, another old friend (v. 10; 11:28), calls in from Judea and is inspired by the everyday sight of Paul's belt (v. 11) to a symbolic action of the type familiar from the Old Testament prophets. The theme is binding—tying up hands and feet, taking away the power of independent action—surely a personal nightmare for the much-travelled and independent Paul. To his friends, Agabus' prophecy is a warning, a timely hint to keep away from danger, to turn and make off in the opposite direction (v. 12). But this personal sense of being 'bound' has been with Paul since 20:22, and he knows, obscurely but ineluctably, that it comes from God. So, gently but firmly, he has to ask his friends to stop crying (v. 13) and let him remain faithful to his calling, even if that means death. For Paul, as for his Master, only one thing matters in the last analysis—that God's will be done (v. 14; compare Luke 22:42).

Caesarea to Jerusalem

The party have their own preparations to make for this last visit to Jerusalem (v. 15). Even their friends in Caesarea seem to be affected by Paul's sombre mood and make sure that Paul is delivered to a safe house in Jerusalem (v. 16). Mnason, a Cypriote with a Greek name, must have been a 'Hellenist', perhaps one of the original Hellenist converts who had left Jerusalem after Stephen's death and so inconspicuously launched the Gentile mission (see 11:19–20). So, for the moment, it's good just to be there and enjoy a warm welcome from these sympathetic friends (v. 17).

PRAYER

Father, keep us faithful to your will, even when the way is dark.

71

PAUL MEETS JAMES

Things have changed since Paul was last in Jerusalem—changed radically since the council met in chapter 15 to find a central platform to hold together Jewish and Gentile Christians in the church.

A change of leadership

Peter, who had faced the struggle to accept his own vision of God's work among Gentiles, and had worked so hard to accommodate the new insights Paul was bringing, has moved on: Luke doesn't mention him after chapter 15. James is now (although Luke never tells us exactly how) in a leadership position in Jerusalem, and it is to James and the elders (v. 18) that Paul brings his delegation, the day after his arrival, to make his report, blow by blow, about what God has been doing through his ministry among the Gentiles (v. 19). There is a clear sense here that Paul has to render account of himself, explain what he has been up to all these years. To understand James' caution, we need to remember that Paul has been effectively a freelance evangelist since his split with Barnabas (15:39), trusting the Spirit's guidance (hence the importance of chapter 16), and (apart from hurriedly touching base in 18:22), setting up his own independent missionary networks. So does he return as hero, or loose cannon?

A change of mood

Formally, James and the elders are full of praise for what God has done through Paul (v. 20), but it becomes clear that the precarious balance held by Peter and James in chapter 15 has been destabilized. Christian opinion has begun to polarize; the church in Jerusalem has been growing, and many of the new believers are deeply suspicious of Paul and everything he stands for. The suspicion is fuelled by 'zeal for the law' (v. 20), a radical fundamentalist stance prepared to impose its will on others, by force if need be. Paul had shared this position in his student days, but that was 20 years ago, and we know from the Jewish historian Josephus that Felix's period of office in Judea saw a massive build-up of fundamentalist fervour and an impassioned rejection of anything that looked like political or religious compromise with Rome. It is also fuelled by misinformation: word has been spreading that Paul's mission is not so much a mission to bring the Gentiles into God's people as a mission to take the Jews out, to persuade Jews to commit apostasy from their ancestral religion (v. 21).

Paul and the law

Watching Paul's progress around Greece and Asia Minor, you could understand how people might think these things about him. Preaching in the synagogue, then engineering a split and walking out with half the congregation, is not a recipe for popularity with community leaders. But what were Paul's converts joining? The apostolic council had established the principle that Gentiles who became Christians did not need to keep the law of Moses (15:19–21), and James has no intention of going back on that pledge (v. 25). But nowhere in Acts does Luke imply that Jews who accepted Jesus as Messiah had to give up keeping the law. In fact, he implies the contrary: Paul's decision to circumcise Timothy (16:3), his continued insistence on visiting synagogues, his keenness to keep Passover and Pentecost (20:6, 16), and the vow at Cenchreae (18:18) all build up to a picture of a Paul who is happy to be regarded—at least when it suits him—as a faithful, Torah-observant Jew (compare 1 Corinthians 9:20).

Building bridges

Now, in order to make it absolutely clear that the charge of teaching apostasy is false, James suggests a neat solution which will demonstrate at a stroke Paul's own devotion to Torah and temple (v. 24) and show his support for the ultra-zealous in a very practical way. Undertaking the voluntary piety of a nazirite vow was an expensive business, and it was common for eminent visitors to make this charitable gesture. James suggests that Paul should pay for the necessary sacrifices for four Christian nazirites (v. 23), and accompany them to the temple while undertaking the ritual purification for himself that was expected for a pious Jew returning from the lands of the Gentiles (v. 24).

PRAYER

Father, as I look back, help me to see not my own successes or failures, but what you have done in and through and in spite of them. And thank you for being with me.

RIOT *in the* TEMPLE

He almost gets away with it! Paul's desire to build bridges with the hardliners of the Jewish-Christian community puts him in a dangerous position, right in the fomenting heart of the city, visiting the temple over a seven-day period (v. 27). It's on the very last day that trouble strikes—trouble that will take Paul eventually to the opposite end of the world.

The Jews from Asia

Agabus had prophesied that Paul would be handed over to the Gentiles by 'the Jews' (21:11), but which Jews? The previous section has shown that the Jerusalem church is not to blame, even if it also reveals a frightening level of hostility there to Paul's mission. One thing Luke's narrative has made clear, though, is that 'the Jews' are not a monochrome group. Here a new group comes into view, the 'Jews from Asia' (v. 27), who see Paul in the temple and jump rapidly to the wrong conclusion. Paul is on dangerous ground now. Bringing Gentiles into the inner court of the temple (v. 28) was a capital offence in Jewish law that was upheld by Roman law. An inscription found in the temple precincts marks the boundary of the Court of the Gentiles and warns that Gentiles may not pass this barrier on pain of death. So Luke is careful to tell us that this part of the charge is simply not true (v. 29). Trophimus of Asia had been seen with Paul in the streets of the city, but Paul had not brought him into the temple. But nobody in this crowd is really interested in finding out the truth. The real charge, far harder to answer, is the charge of 'teaching everyone everywhere against the people, the law and this place' (v. 28). The immediate result is that Paul is physically ejected from the centre of worship and 'the doors were shut' (v. 30)—a note of finality, marking the end of an era in Paul's life, and a moment of deep irony for this visionary preacher who had dedicated his life to breaking down the barriers that religious people put up around their faith.

The tribune of the cohort

Paul has no time to reflect on the irony of his situation. He is within an ace of receiving the same kind of summary execution he had seen meted out on Stephen (7:54–60) when word gets back to the Roman military commander in charge of policing the temple area (v. 31). Romans were not allowed inside the inner courts of the temple, but they were very concerned to keep an eye on this volatile spot, especially at festival times, and had built a fortress, the Antonia, right on the corner of the temple precinct to give them a commanding position over what was happening inside. Here is another irony: by locking Paul out of the inner courts, the rioters have brought him into the domain controlled by the imperial power of Rome (v. 32), and it is this power that now takes charge of Paul.

The young officer who clatters down the steps of the Antonia with his squaddies undoubtedly saves Paul's life (vv. 33–36), but the chains they place on Paul will not come off (except briefly when Paul is facing his accusers) for the rest of the book.

A citizen of no mean city

There's a nice John Buchan touch about the next scene. To the bored young tribune on temple guard duty—just as to the young British or US soldier in the Middle East—all orientals look the same. The man at the centre of the riot has got to be some kind of terrorist. The 'Egyptian' (v. 38) was just one of the many religious agitators who were giving Rome grief in those unsettled years leading up to the Jewish war with Rome. According to Josephus (*Antiquities* 20:169–72; *Jewish War* 2:261–63), an Egyptian claiming to be a prophet had recently led a mob to the Mount of Olives to watch the walls of Jerusalem fall. The governor Felix dispersed the mob with the aid of soldiers, but the ringleader escaped. Not unnaturally, the tribune here thinks he's struck lucky. So when this dishevelled figure addresses him politely in faultless Greek (v. 37), the effect is something like the whirling dervish in a John Buchan novel speaking in an impeccable Oxford accent. There's a serious side to the exchange, however. Faced with the brutality of empire, Paul displays a calm dignity that impresses the tribune. The momentary respite gives Paul the chance to make his last formal address to the people of Jerusalem, standing on the steps like a Greek orator (v. 40).

PRAYER
Father, teach us to find our dignity and status only in you.

PAUL *the* JEW

There is a certain farcical element in Paul's position here, pinned down outside the sanctuary, halfway up the steps of the fortress, brandished aloft by Roman soldiers with the mob clutching at him below. But the farce also underlines Paul's marginal status, not only physically but politically and culturally. It was perhaps part of the secret of his success as a missionary that Paul was able to move effortlessly between the three aspects of his identity—Jewish, Greek and Roman. In the next few scenes he will need to deploy all of those—and remain true to his underlying calling as a disciple of Jesus Christ.

Brothers and fathers

Paul the Jew comes first (21:39), proudly stated at this focal point of Jewish identity. As a Jew, he has a right to be in the temple, and to address the crowd in their own language (21:40, 22:2), which the Roman tribune can never share. Paul may have been raised in a Greek city, but he is determined to show that his Hebrew credentials are second to none (compare Philippians 3:4–6). This is the first of Paul's defence speeches in Acts, but it is not the kind of self-defence we might expect. There is no reasoned, point-by-point rebuttal of the charges laid against him in 21:28. Instead, he goes right back to his own starting points, seeking to make his audience understand the whole life-journey that has brought him to where he is now. So the speech begins by laying out in relentless detail how much Paul shares with his audience (vv. 1–5): Jewish first and foremost, born in Tarsus, educated in Jerusalem at the feet of one of the century's most revered saints and scholars, and sharing the same zeal that fires up his audience.

Who are you, Lord?

The key to understanding his present predicament, though, lies in a moment of vision on the Damascus road, that encounter with the living Lord that turned his life around for ever (v. 6). It was precisely the same 'zeal' that the audience shares that made him a persecutor (vv. 4–5) and brought him face-to-face with the crucified Jesus, surrounded by the bright light of heaven (vv. 7–8). If we compare Paul's retelling here with chapter 9, we can see that different details are emphasized for the different occasions. Here the story is told from Paul's viewpoint, so we don't see Ananias' personal doubts and prevarications (9:10–16). Paul simply stresses Ananias' piety and his good standing in the Jewish community (v. 12). What is important is that Paul's Lord is not some new deity but 'the God of our fathers' (v. 14), who has chosen Saul for a purpose (v. 10).

I will send you far away

What that purpose is becomes clear only gradually. The fundamental shape of this experience for Paul—as for Isaiah and all the prophets—is an encounter with the living God. It's about being chosen to know God's will, to see God's Righteous One, to hear a voice from his mouth (v. 14). The commission grows out of that encounter: you can't be a witness (v. 15) unless you have first seen and heard for yourself, experienced something of the glory of heaven (v. 11), and let it knock you off your high horse (v. 7). Everything else stems from that initial encounter: first, incorporation into a new community (v. 16), a letting go of the past and a humble acceptance of a new identity, then repeatedly being drawn back to worship and prayer (vv. 17–18), a need to be in God's presence simply because God is worth it—which is what worship is about. Then (and only then) comes a new direction, a step at a time: first recognizing the impossibility of going on any further, then facing up honestly to the past (vv. 19–20), and finally a new direction for the future (v. 21).

REFLECTION

'Evangelism is useless unless it is the work of one devoted to God, willing and glad to suffer all things for God, penetrated by the attractiveness of God.'

Evelyn Underhill

STATUS GAMES

Paul has done very well so far, travelling around the empire and using its resources without drawing official attention to himself (apart from a few local skirmishes). Here, however, on the temple steps, he has finally run out of options. He has to play the only trump he's got, and trust God for the outcome.

Away with him!

Up to this point, the crowd has been listening in spellbound silence. The zealot who unexpectedly meets his God, the heavenly voice, the prophetic call—all this can be fitted into the mould of preconceived ideas. But the word 'Gentiles' (v. 21) acts like a red rag to this bullish, militant crowd. The idea that God should reveal himself to his faithful followers is conceivable; that the revelation in some way includes the Gentiles is not (v. 22)—not, that is, to this particular brand of fundamentalism. It was not inconceivable to first-century Judaism in general that God's revelation to Israel should be for the sake of the outside world. In fact, the burden of Acts is that Paul's vision is not only consistent with scripture but is an organic outworking of God's self-revelation to Israel. But alongside the argument (which is worked out in detail in this series of trial scenes), Luke also shows us a progressive rejection of that insight by successive groups, culminating in the expulsion of Paul's message from the heart of his own tradition.

Out of the frying-pan into the fire

The Roman officer has been standing by all this time, unable to understand Paul's speech but carefully watching the body language of the crowd—which suddenly erupts (v. 23). Now he decides it's time to intervene. He hasn't a clue what Paul was talking about, but it was obviously inflammatory, so the squaddies are ordered to interrogate the prisoner to find out what's going on (v. 24). Given the routine brutality of army interrogation of foreign nationals, Paul's 'rescue' is rather like falling out of the frying-pan into the fire. So he decides to play his trump card, and reveals to the horrified centurion that he has arrested a Roman citizen (vv. 25–26). This is a bit like having a suspected terrorist suddenly whipping out a US passport.

There's a touch of farce about the whole scene, as the embarrassed tribune falls back from the forcible interrogation (v. 29)—but still does not release Paul.

This man is a Roman

We might perhaps ask why Paul has waited till this moment to reveal his Roman citizenship to the tribune. Things have been happening rather fast, though, and outside, on the steps before the hostile crowd in the temple, it was more important for Paul to focus on his Jewish identity. In private, inside the Roman fortress, things are rather different, and Paul has to face up to the fact that he is now, for good or ill, in Roman custody. That situation has to be played with care. The empire could function quite usefully to protect its citizens from local injustice, but its legal machinery was relentless, and no one would want to get into it unless they were sure they had a way out. For provincials, being a Roman citizen (a comparatively rare privilege at this date) meant two things. It meant they could not be beaten, bound or executed without a fair trial, and that their accusers had to appear in person to lay charges against them. It also meant that they had the right to appeal to have their case heard before the emperor in Rome—and, as we shall see, this is the right that Paul will eventually invoke when he stands before Festus (25:9–12).

Born or bought?

There is a nice irony in the exchange with the tribune in verse 28. For Paul, the privilege of citizenship could be taken for granted as part of his family history, whereas the tribune has to confess that his own citizen rank is of much more recent origin. So the status levels of officer and prisoner are in one sense reversed, although the prisoner remains in custody. The exchange has sown enough doubt in the tribune's mind to leave him seriously worried (v. 29). Detaining a citizen without formal charge could be a very serious mistake, which could have repercussions in the highest quarters. On the other hand, failing to detain a terrorist could have equally serious repercussions.

PRAYER

Pray for soldiers, police officers, prison guards, and all whose jobs give them control over the lives of others.

75   ACTS 22:30—23:9

BEFORE *the* SANHEDRIN

From the rioting zealots in the temple to the heart of a corrupt colonial administration: Luke shows us here a Paul who is poised between the two extremes of pre-war Jerusalem, desperately trying to offer both sides a vision of a different future.

Judicial enquiry

The tribune's next step is logical enough. Paul must have done something illegal to have caused so much disturbance, so, since there is clearly no hope of getting a rational answer from the temple crowd, he needs to get the prisoner examined by the Sanhedrin, the ruling council of Judea and the only native body with which the Roman government could do business (v. 30). This is not, strictly speaking, a trial. It is a judicial enquiry on the tribune's behalf, set up to ascertain if there is actually any charge to answer. The effect, for Luke's readers, is twofold. It underlines the parallels with the trials of Jesus (compare Luke 22:66; 23:13), and it ensures that Paul gets his chance to make a second *apologia* or defence speech before a different Jerusalem group—the chief priests and other leaders who had made such a dramatic impact on the Jerusalem apostles 20 years before (see 4:6, 23; 5:24). Like other contemporary writers, Luke speaks of 'high priests' in the plural because, although there was only one high priest in office at a time, retired high priests retained their title and much of their influence until their death.

Before the council

The atmosphere of the council chamber should have been very different from that of the temple mob. Paul addresses the council as 'brothers' (v. 1)—that is, as equals—and begins his speech by stressing how much he and they have in common. He has nothing to be ashamed of: everything he has done to date has been done in good conscience as a loyal and observant Jew, conducting his life in a way that is loyal to God. It is a bold claim, and the high priest regards it as provocative (v. 2). Ananias was a controversial figure who earned a name for exceptional wealth (and exceptional greed) in the turbulent years leading up to the outbreak of the Jewish War, and was eventu-

170

ally assassinated by rebels on the outbreak of war in AD66 (Josephus, *Jewish War* 2.429, 441–42). For Luke's readers, as for Paul himself, Ananias would have been an ambivalent figure, representing by virtue of his office the highest and holiest religious authority in Judaism, yet widely known for venality and corruption—a 'whitewashed wall' (v. 3) concealing inner depths of corruption.

Allies and enemies

The action of ordering Paul to be struck on the mouth tips what should have been an orderly debate over the edge into an undignified fracas. Paul reacts with anger, but takes the opportunity to claim the moral high ground and shows himself well-trained in legal argumentation (vv. 3–4). Ananias' action could have no legal justification, and so he shows himself unworthy to be regarded as a 'ruler of the people' (v. 5, quoting Exodus 22:28). Almost inevitably, then, Paul looks around and decides he has no chance of getting a fair hearing from this council. His only hope is to appeal over the heads of the priestly hierarchy to other members of the Sanhedrin (and beyond them, perhaps, to the wider community) by aligning himself with his natural allies, the Pharisees (v. 6).

Pharisees and Sadducees differed on many points of interpretation of the scriptures. The Sadducees were conservatives who held that only a literal interpretation of scripture was acceptable. They held to Torah only, devalued the Prophets and Writings, and regarded the idea of resurrection (which was a commonly held belief in first-century Judaism) as a new and unscriptural doctrine. But we should not regard Paul's appeal to the resurrection simply as a cynical ploy to divide the assembly. It allows Paul to swing the argument back to his own agenda (compare 26:8), and reminds his audience—and Luke's readers—that there is a real theological issue at stake here (v. 9). The Pharisees believed (unlike the Sadducees) that God was still revealing himself to his people. The real question was, were they prepared to accept that the apostolic testimony to Christ was part of this continuing self-revelation?

PRAYER

Pray for lawyers, judges, court officials, and all to whom the administration of justice is entrusted.

76 ACTS 23:10–30

PLOTS & COUNTERPLOTS

The scene is confused and confusing—but it must have been even more confusing for Paul, kept in the dark and knowing nothing of what was going on. Luckily for him, Someone else did...

Take courage

Paul's outburst has the effect of splitting the council into factions and starting a major riot. Certainly that's what it sounds like to the tribune, listening outside (v. 10), so he sends the troops down to rescue Paul and take him back to the fortress.

It's precisely at this point of maximum confusion, in the darkness of uncertainty, danger, instability and the loss of personhood, that 'the Lord stood by him' (v. 11). Paul must have been wondering whether his predicament meant that God had abandoned him. Was he wrong to come back to Jerusalem? Was it crazy to go along with James' proposal and carry out the temple ritual—which is what he'd been doing only 36 hours before? More importantly, was his whole mission based on false premises? Bravado is all very well (and Paul was obviously the kind of person who thrived on confrontation), but in the long, slow reaches of the night, it's easy to wonder if we've got it all wrong. So this is a crucial reassurance from the Lord, both for Paul and for us as readers: 'Don't worry; everything that's happening is part of *my* plan.'

As the action speeds up, Luke really slows down his narrative pace in this section, so we can follow every twist in an increasingly convoluted plot and overhear every whispered conversation. It's as if he's saying, 'How on earth is God going to get Paul out of this one? Just watch and wonder!'

Ambush in the temple

The first step in getting Paul out of Jerusalem is an apparent disaster, but disasters in Acts have a way of furthering God's own plan. As long as Paul is in the Antonia fortress, he's safe, but he can't stay there for ever. So a small group of conspirators (vv. 12–13) make a plan to ambush Paul and take summary action the next time the Romans bring him down through the temple precincts to meet the Sanhedrin. The plotters are worryingly close to elements in the council itself

(vv. 14–15), some of whom could have seen this as a useful strategy to circumvent the Roman legal stranglehold that prevented them from carrying their own legal processes to their logical conclusion. There is clearly a strong element in Jerusalem who are convinced that Paul is an incurable apostate who must be removed for the sake of Israel's purity. But not all the young radicals milling around in the crowd are hostile to Paul, and he has a young nephew who overhears the plot and spills the beans to the tribune (vv. 16–22). This is the first time we've heard that Paul has a sister, but this could partly explain the constant pressures that keep drawing him back to Jerusalem.

From Jerusalem to Caesarea

Now matters are in the tribune's hands, and his duty is clear. As a Roman citizen, Paul is entitled to a fair trial, and it is becoming clear that he won't get that in Jerusalem. The only option is to get him out of the city, fast, with an armed, mounted escort (vv. 23–24). The tribune's nervousness is palpable, as is his determination to get Paul off his own patch and safely into Roman custody. The Antonia is little more than a fortified police station, and the last thing he wants is a mob trying to storm his gates. But the prisoner must be accompanied by a letter of explanation (vv. 25–30), and this has to be composed with some care: no need to mention that unfortunate business about trying to flog Paul before he let on that he was a Roman (v. 27). The letter formally proclaims Paul's innocence under Roman law (v. 29), although it acknowledges that he may still have a charge to answer under Jewish law (v. 30).

The tribune (now identified as Claudias Lysias) is evidently convinced that there is no substance in the original charge of violating the sanctity of the temple precincts by bringing a Gentile into the Court of Israel (21:28). In any case, under Roman law a citizen could not be brought to trial unless his accusers were there in person to lay charges, and there is no sign that anyone is prepared to do that. What remains is the more general charge of teaching against the law and the temple (21:28), and that is the case Lysias is transferring to the jurisdiction of Felix—provided Paul's accusers are prepared to travel to Caesarea to make their case before the governor (v. 30).

PRAYER

Pray for all who feel abandoned by family, friends, society.

TRIAL *in* CAESAREA

Now the stage shifts from the explosive atmosphere of Jerusalem to the seat of Roman provincial government in Caesarea. Felix (unlike Claudius Lysias) is on his home ground, hearing the case before his own tribunal, and the burden of proof has shifted to the accusers—hence the change of tone.

Down to Caesarea

The amount of detail in this story is extraordinary. God's rescue mission now enlists (unwittingly) not only the tribune but two centurions, 200 soldiers, 70 cavalrymen and 200 spearmen (23:23), all clattering down to Antipatris at dead of night (v. 31). This is the only place in his travels where Paul is described as riding (which rather implies that it was unusual). Antipatris was a day's march from Jerusalem on foot, so the foot-soldiers return to Jerusalem the next day (v. 32). But it's an easy ride for the cavalrymen, who act as an escort to deliver Paul safely to Felix the governor in Caesarea (v. 33). This is a significant move, down from the uplands of Judea to the Mediterranean coast, out from the political control of the temple hierarchy (where even the tribune has to move circumspectly) to a more public arena, and securely into colonial territory. Caesarea Maritima was a cosmopolitan Greek city, where Jews were a vocal but not dominant segment of the population. More importantly for Paul, it was also the seat of the Roman administration's provincial HQ, so Paul is coming closer and closer to the seat of Roman power.

Meet the governor

The first step is for the escort to hand Paul over, complete with attached letter, to the Roman magistrate in whose hands (humanly speaking) his future lies (v. 33). On the face of it, it is a rather dubious prospect. Felix (23:24) was a slave in origin, who, with his brother Pallas, became a confidant and favourite at the imperial court. As a mark of favour, the emperor Claudius made him procurator of Judea (around AD52–60), much to the disgust of the later Roman historian Tacitus, who described Felix as wielding the power of a king 'with all cruelty and lust, and with the mentality of a slave' (Tacitus, *Histories*

5.9). It was during Felix's procuratorship that the province of Judea began to move inexorably towards revolt against Rome.

Felix's first question is, on the face of it, an odd one: 'What province are you from?' (v. 34). The answer might have given him the option of transferring the case to the prisoner's home province, but Paul's home province of Cilicia, like Judea, falls under the ultimate jurisdiction of the legate of Syria, so there is no easy way out there. Felix will have to hear the case himself (v. 35).

The case for the prosecution

The accusers have to present their case in person, and in five days' time, a deputation from the Sanhedrin duly arrives, together with a carefully briefed Greek orator (no expense spared!) to ensure that the case is presented to the governor in the most advantageous way possible (v. 1). Tertullus' speech (vv. 2–8) is couched in the best rhetorical style, nicely calculated to win friends and influence people. In fact, almost half the speech (as Luke reports it) is taken up with flattery, stressing (against all the evidence, it must be said) Felix's record of peaceful political reform, his political sagacity and his excellent reputation. Tertullus then moves to setting out the charges against Paul in terms designed to impress a Roman governor: provoking civil riots (*staseis*) among Jews throughout the inhabited world (v. 5), and being a ringleader of the Nazarean sect. Then comes the more specific charge of profaning the temple by taking Gentiles past the permitted limits (v. 6). That's the capital charge; that's the one that should stick—apart from the minor technicality that it wasn't the Sanhedrin who originally apprehended Paul, and the Asian pilgrims who raised the original hue and cry in the temple are not here to press the charge.

PRAYER

Pray for all prisoners and captives, all refugees and asylum seekers, all who feel confused, outmanoeuvred and overwhelmed by the forces of officialdom.

78

COURTROOM DRAMA

All the speeches in Acts address two audiences: the immediate audience inside the dramatic scene as it unfolds, and the wider audience of Luke's readers. This one is no exception. Paul is making his *apologia*, the speech for the defence (v. 10), using all the wits God gave him to talk his way out of trouble. But he is also offering a defence of a whole way of life, a Way that some people call a 'sect' (v. 14), but which for Paul (and for Luke) is simply the logical outcome of his ancestral faith. So, like all the speeches in this final section of Acts, this one serves both as legal defence and as the affirmation and confirmation of the gospel itself (compare Philippians 1:7, 16). As we watch and listen to the courtroom drama, Luke is asking us to do two things: to weigh up an argument, and to empathize with a person—a person facing the greatest challenge of his life.

The case for the defence

On the one hand are the men in suits: official deputations, expensive barristers, the best that money can buy. On the other, there is just the prisoner, wearing the clothes he stands up in (he didn't expect to be arrested the day he set out for the temple), speaking (as was normal in a Roman court) in his own defence. Paul knew that you had to treat the Roman governor with respect if you were going to get anywhere. Tertullus' speech in verses 2–4 was a piece of unabashed flattery. Paul plays the same game, but plays it by his own rules. 'I understand,' he begins (with all the dignity of an outraged citizen of cosmopolitan Tarsus), 'that you have been judge over this nation for many years' (v. 10). It's hardly fulsome, but it fulfils the protocols of politeness and allows Paul to move on to a careful statement of the facts, which just as carefully avoids engaging with the accusation except on his own terms.

Let's get the facts straight

Can it really be only twelve days (v. 11) since Paul travelled up to Jerusalem, back in 21:15? It was, Paul maintains, a perfectly legitimate journey, made for the entirely pious and proper purpose of worshipping in Jerusalem, and with no intention of getting into disputes or rabble-rousing either in the synagogues or in the city (v. 12). Paul is, of course, being quite truthful here (if a little economical). He has done plenty of disputing in synagogues across Asia, Macedonia and Achaea, but not in Jerusalem; and under Roman law the original plaintiffs have to be present to press the charge (vv. 13, 19).

The Way that they call a sect

All I have done, Paul says, is to follow my ancestral religion according to this Way, a Way that makes me more faithful, not less, to the scriptures we share (v. 14). Some people call it a 'sect', but that just means 'choice'. First-century Judaism was not monolithic: it offered choices, different party allegiances, different emphases in the interpretation of the common heritage. One of the main differences, we already know: Pharisees and Sadducees differed in their interpretation of the scriptural witness to resurrection (vv. 15, 21; 23:6–8). But these are choices to be made within Judaism, legitimate ways of being Jewish—and so, Paul implies, is the Way I have chosen, the Way that sharpens my conscience and makes me ever more acutely aware of the duty I owe both to God and to my neighbour (v. 16). So it is a logical outcome of this shared faith that brings Paul back to the temple after many years (v. 17) and leads to his being found there, not desecrating the temple but completing a rite of purification (v. 18).

The reference to 'offerings' (v. 17) would not have made much sense to Felix; Luke seems here to be combining the story of the nazirite vow (which Paul took on after his arrival in Jerusalem: 21:23–24) and the collection for the Jerusalem church, which we only know of from his letters (see Romans 15:25–28).

REFLECTION

'Do not fear what they fear, and do not be intimidated, but in your hearts sanctify Christ as Lord. Always be ready to make your defence to anyone who demands from you an accounting for the hope that is in you; yet do it with gentleness and reverence.'

1 Peter 3:14–16

79

ACTS 24:22—25:12

'I APPEAL *to* CAESAR'

And after all the drama? Nothing but the worst kind of waiting, waiting with no end in view, waiting on the whim of an official bureaucracy over which we have no control whatever. Waiting can sap our reserves of faith and courage like nothing else can.

Procrastination of a procurator

Felix is intrigued, but undecided. He already knows a bit about this Way, Luke tells us (v. 22: we have to wait till verse 24 to find out why), but he has received two conflicting accounts of the temple riot, and he won't make a legal decision till Lysias the tribune comes down to give a full report. Presumably the deputation from the Sanhedrin is allowed to go back to Jerusalem, but Paul remains in custody in the *praetorium* of Herod (23:35). At first, it probably doesn't seem too bad: Paul is given some liberty within the prison, and his friends and family are allowed to minister to him by providing food and clothing (v. 23). Within a few days, Felix is back, this time with his wife Drusilla, who was the younger daughter of Herod Agrippa I. Drusilla's knowledge of Jewish affairs could well account for Felix's interest in Paul's case, and for his frequent visits to converse with Paul (v. 26). But the couple's interest is strictly limited: when religion gets up close and personal, it's time to back off. Paul's talk about the moral demands of religion (v. 25) is much too close for comfort to Felix. So the case remains unresolved. Bribery would have been one (strictly illegal) way out, but Paul won't play that game (v. 26). Meanwhile, the days and weeks are ticking away.

New man in town

Paul has been in prison for a full two years when Felix's term of office comes to an end. He leaves Paul in prison (v. 27), and it is left to the new governor, Porcius Festus, to clear out his predecessor's filing-cabinet. Porcius Festus succeeded Felix as procurator about AD60, and vainly did his best to reverse the slide into anarchy that had begun under Felix. An early meeting with the ruling council in Jerusalem would have been a good way to start (v. 1), and listening carefully to a long-standing complaint would make a good impression

(v. 2). But Festus is careful not to get too closely identified with the interests of the temple hierarchy, and insists that if the case is to be reopened it will be heard in Caesarea (vv. 4–5).

The second hearing in Caesarea

Once again, Paul and his accusers are summoned to appear at the governor's tribunal (v. 6), not so much to hear the case as to determine if there is a case to answer and, if so, who should act as judge. Once again, the prosecution and defence state their cases (vv. 7–8). Now Festus sees an obvious way of clearing his backlog and ingratiating himself with the provincials at a stroke: why not send the case to be tried in Jerusalem (v. 9)? This means removing the case from Roman jurisdiction and treating it as a problem under Jewish law— although Festus intends to retain some kind of presence in the process. Because Paul is a Roman citizen, though, Festus cannot make this decision for him. He has to ask if Paul is willing to be tried in Jerusalem. If Paul had accepted the jurisdiction of the local court, he would have been bound by its verdict. But no governor had the power to compel him to accept its jurisdiction. That was one of the privileges of the citizen.

To Festus, it must have looked straightforward enough: the temple riot was a long way in the past. But Paul knows that the passions roused by his visit to Jerusalem are still seething just under the surface (v. 3). Sending him to Jerusalem would be, effectively, to sign his death warrant. So he has only one option left: to appeal to have his case heard in Rome, at the tribunal of Caesar himself (v. 11). This is not about appealing against a verdict (as in modern English law) but about the fundamental right to decide where and under what system of jurisdiction his case will be heard. The outcome is still very much in the balance: 'You have appealed to Caesar: to Caesar you shall go' (v. 12).

REFLECTION

'The big courage is the cold-blooded kind, the kind that never lets go even when you're feeling empty inside, and your blood's thin, and the trouble's not over in an hour or two but lasts for months and years… I reckon fortitude's the biggest thing a man can have… [And] the head man at the job was the Apostle Paul…'

Buchan, (n.d.), pp. 631–32

POWER POLITICS

Luke takes a lot of trouble here, setting the scene for the last big speech in Paul's protracted self-defence. It's like a stage setting, with the bustle and buzz of the actors assembling for the last big courtroom scene, and Luke the master storyteller makes the most of it. But the story has its place in history too, and we need a few programme notes at this point to explain things that would have been perfectly familiar to Luke's first readers.

Paul and the Roman citizenship

The whole story turns on Paul's claim to be a Roman citizen, which provides the mechanism (humanly speaking) for getting Paul out of Jerusalem and off to Rome. Paul does not mention his Roman status in his letters, but there is no obvious reason why he should mention this fact of family history in his letters to fellow Christians. It was only relevant, as here, in a dispute over identity before a Roman magistrate.

How did someone prove their citizen status? Recently enfranchised citizens, like the veterans who regularly received their citizenship on discharge from the Roman army, would be given a *diploma* to prove it, a folded bronze (or lead) tablet that could be easily carried around. But for second- or third-generation citizens, like Paul, the question of proof was less likely to arise in the normal circumstances of provincial life, and the record would simply be kept in the citizen-lists of the citizen's native town, which were updated every five years for tax registration purposes. But given that magistrates could be sued for mistreating a Roman citizen, someone in Paul's position could simply rely on the magistrate's constant fear of litigation. Court cases from disgruntled citizens could do a lot of damage to a rising political career, and it was always wiser to play safe.

Festus, Agrippa and Bernice

Who are the players in this final scene? Festus, the new governor, is busily putting his house in order and energetically clearing his desk for the new administration. The case of *Paul v. Sanhedrin* has to be transferred to Rome, and he will have to provide some paperwork to send with the prisoner (vv. 26–27). Meanwhile, all the protocols of political politeness have to go on—and here come the local royalty, King Agrippa and his consort Bernice, paying a courtesy call to welcome the new governor (v. 13). There is a nice touch of court scandal about these new arrivals, which would not have been lost on Luke's first readers. Agrippa II was the son of Agrippa I (the 'Herod' of Acts 12). He had an uneasy relationship with the Jerusalem hierarchy in the years before the war, and ended his days in Rome. Bernice was his sister (and also the sister of Felix's wife Drusilla), and caused a scandal by coming to live with her brother after the death of her previous husband, their uncle Herod of Chalcis. Nobody was quite sure of the relationship between Agrippa and Bernice, although most people thought the worst. To Festus, the royal couple was an important part of the local political scene, with the potential to become valuable allies or dangerous antagonists.

Conversations in court

Luke gives the impression that Festus is trying desperately to find something to entertain his visitors when Paul's case comes up in conversation (v. 14). Whatever the reason, it attracts Agrippa's attention (v. 22), and it is entirely plausible that the incoming governor, new to Jewish politics and politely puzzled by Jewish religious rivalries, should enlist the aid of this local potentate in drafting his letter to the emperor (vv. 26–27). It gives him the chance to make a good propaganda point about Roman standards of justice and fair play (v. 16). But Festus' conversation also gives us, as readers, a behind-the-scenes glimpse of the Roman view of the whole proceedings (vv. 18–21, 24–25). Like Gallio before him (18:14–15), this Roman governor cannot see that Paul has committed any offence against Roman law. It's all a matter of academic disputes about the native superstition (*deisidaimonia*, a very dismissive term) and about some dead guy called Jesus whom Paul maintains is alive (v. 19). This is not a bad summary of what Paul's life was all about!

REFLECTION

'It is my eager expectation and hope that… by my speaking with all boldness, Christ will be exalted now as always in my body, whether by life or by death. For to me, living is Christ, and dying is gain' (Philippians 1:20–21). What's the one sentence by which you would like an observer to sum up your life?

The HEAVENLY VISION

The scene is set; the audience is assembled; the performance is about to begin. All we need is the soloist, summoned from prison to give the performance of his life. That's precisely what this is: Paul's last big speech in Acts, the final aria into which Luke pours his own summing-up of what Paul's mission—Paul's whole life—adds up to. And it all goes back to that Damascus road encounter, to the vision of Christ that gives meaning to the whole.

The prophet and the king

Festus has had his say, and the Roman viewpoint now fades into the background. Luke's narrative spotlight focuses all our attention on the two central players, Paul and Agrippa (v. 1). Paul makes it very clear from the outset that he is addressing his longest and most impassioned defence speech to 'King Agrippa' (v. 2), and he reiterates the address at key points in the speech (vv. 7, 13, 19, 26–29). Agrippa was a polit-ical ally of Rome, but he is also and more importantly invoked as an expert in Jewish law (v. 3), with a good record of support for Jewish political interests in Rome. In his official capacity, he has ultimate responsibility for the running of the temple and the appointment of the high priest, so he is a significant player in Jewish affairs, both in Jerusalem and in the diaspora. So, with Festus looking on, Paul's argu-ment is predominantly a conversation within the Jewish community. In that context, Paul adopts the biblical stance of the prophet, acting out of faithfulness to God's call, issuing a disturbing personal challenge to the king. Prophets who talk that way to kings need one characteristic above all: *parrhesia* (26:26), a word we often translate as 'boldness' but which carries with it all the overtones of Athenian free speech and the integrity of the philosopher confronting the wielders of absolute power with a few home truths (see comment on 4:13–31).

Following the Way

'Tell us about yourself,' says Agrippa (v. 1), and that is precisely what Paul does. It's all about 'my way of life' as an observant Jew growing up in Jerusalem (v. 4). Tarsus and Rome recede into the background; this is what really counts. That life, says Paul, is its own testimony, publicly known and uncontested (v. 5)—the life of a Pharisee, devoted to the most stringent interpretation of the Jewish heritage. And it's that shared heritage, not some alien outside influence—that biblical treasury of promise and hope—that underlies where he is today. There is a real continuity, Paul is arguing, between the Pharisee and the apostle, and the thread that ties them together is the shared hope in the resurrection of the dead. In theory, Paul implies, we are all committed to the belief that God raises the dead (v. 8). The trouble is, we seem very reluctant to admit that what we believe in might actually be true.

Who are you, Lord?

Now we're coming to the point—that foundational vision to which Paul keeps returning and which gives meaning to his whole life. We know the story already (chs. 9; 21), but note the extra vividness in this description, the visual detail ('brighter than the midday sun') that we haven't heard before (v. 13). It's as if Paul, forced into inactivity in prison, has been drawn further and further back to reliving the ground-breaking encounter that has brought him to where he is today. He has been reflecting on its deeper meaning: 'it is hard for you to kick against the ox-goad' (v. 14) was a proverbial saying in Greek, expressing the futility of resisting the divine imperative. This is the central challenge of Acts, expressed in a variety of ways by characters from all sides of the debate (see 5:39; 15:10): how can anyone resist the inbreaking activity of God's spirit?

For Paul himself, the challenge came with the profoundly destabilizing realization of precisely whom his violent, intolerant zeal was really directed against (v. 15). Yet that moment of truth formed the ground— the only ground—on which he could stand on his feet (v. 16) and face the future. Moreover, this vision wasn't a one-off, but an introduction to a living presence (v. 16). Witness isn't just about looking back, but about looking forward to what God is going to go on revealing in our lives.

PRAYER

Thanks be to thee, my Lord Jesus Christ, for all the benefits thou hast
won for me, for all the pains and insults thou hast borne for me.
O most merciful Redeemer, friend and brother, may I know thee more
clearly, love thee more dearly, and follow thee more nearly, day by day.

St Richard of Chichester

ALMOST PERSUADED

Light to the Gentiles

Paul's vision isn't a punishment or even just a warning, but a commission and a promise (v. 16)—the clearest statement yet that Paul saw his vision on the Damascus road as a prophetic call to bring the gospel to the Gentiles (compare Galatians 1:15–16). The calling is couched in the language of Isaiah (see Isaiah 42:7, 16; 49:6) and, for Luke's readers, echoes the prophetic vision of Simeon in Luke 2:32. Here Paul expresses (with hindsight, surely) the comprehensive and unambiguous vision into which his whole life's work has been leading, extending to the Gentiles—that is, to the whole world— what was already on offer to Israel: light, the kingdom of God, the remission of sins, and a share in the world to come (v. 18). The offer is the same for everybody, Jew and Gentile alike. And the conditions are exactly the same, for Gentile as for Jew: repentance and faith in the name of Jesus, the Persecuted One who speaks from heaven. So Festus was right. It is all about this dead guy called Jesus (25:19), whom Paul had experienced as a living presence.

Here I stand

'After that, King Agrippa, I was not disobedient to the heavenly vision' (v. 19)—and that, of course, is the crunch. As Agrippa knows (and as Greek philosophers like Socrates knew), you don't just walk away from that kind of revelation. Looking back, Paul sees his whole missionary enterprise, the story unfolded by Luke step by step through the second half of Acts, springing from that moment (vv. 19–20). That's what brought him to the point of arrest in the temple (v. 21); that's the ground on which he makes his stand (v. 22). And that's the final note of *apologia* from this very undefensive defendant: 'However you cut it, this is my testimony; this is what I have to say to great and small alike.' There's nothing outlandish about this testimony, nothing alien to what Moses and the prophets have led us to expect. If we read them properly (that is, if we read them in the way Luke's narrative has trained us to do: see Luke 24:26, 46; Acts 3:18; 17:3), the scriptures reveal a Christ who accepts the burden and fragility of human suffering, and in doing so releases life and light both to the Jewish people and to the rest of the world (v. 23).

Do you believe?

As a legal defence, this speech is a washout. Its only effect is to convince Festus that Paul is a harmless nutcase (v. 24)—which may be no bad thing in legal terms (vv. 31–32), but hardly constitutes a serious *apologia* to the Roman emperor.

The real issue is not self-defence, but faith, and in the vivid dialogue that closes the scene (vv. 26–29), Paul's passionate conviction almost leaps off the page. This is a direct, prophetic appeal to the king, which at the same time breaks down the barriers between the dramatic audience (the 'on-stage' audience listening to Paul's speech) and the real-world audience of the readers. Suddenly, this isn't just an entertaining way to pass the afternoon: it's a story that has the potential to change lives. Paul appeals to Agrippa to consider the real, personal import of the story he has just heard, a double appeal to the publicly known facts of the story (v. 26) and to the scriptural framework that unlocks the events' true significance (v. 27). Its object is clear: Agrippa is right, Paul is doing his best to make him a Christian (v. 28)—him and anyone else who hears (or reads) this remarkable story (v. 29). This is surely as broad a hint as we could hope for of Luke's underlying purpose in writing: narrative and speech combine to show us the unfolding events and to spell out their hidden significance. The ultimate aim of studying the scriptures is persuasion—persuasion leading to faith.

REFLECTION

'We proclaim Christ crucified, a stumbling-block to Jews and foolishness to Gentiles, but to those who are the called, both Jews and Greeks, Christ the power of God and the wisdom of God.'

1 Corinthians 1:23–24

83

DOWN *to the* SEA *in* SHIPS

After the long build-up of tension, the charge and counter-charge of courtroom rhetoric, and the frustrations of two years' imprisonment, it's a relief to be on the move again. This final voyage to Rome is a journey long planned (19:21) and underwritten by God's promise (23:11), but not at all the way Paul had envisaged it. Paul is still in chains, in the grip of forces outside his control, shipped from place to place like a parcel (v. 1)—very different from his earlier voyages as a freewheeling traveller. But he has the reassurance that the real power controlling his movements is not the imperial bureaucracy but the plan of God.

Under way

Even in human terms, he is not alone on this final voyage. Look at the dynamic interplay of verbs in verse 1: first, the impersonal language of bureaucracy ('it was decided'—by Them Upstairs, by the unknown forces that control our destiny); then, the warmth of companionship ('that we should sail'—don't worry, you've got friends coming with you). Companionship makes all the difference (compare the poignant notes in Paul's prison letters: Colossians 4:14; 2 Timothy 4:11). God's guiding hand can be seen even in the detail. Julius the centurion, evidently a decent professional soldier trying to do a decent job, provides a human face within the system (vv. 1, 3). Aristarchus of Thessalonica (v. 2) has been one of the party since 19:29 (see Colossians 4:10). But we can also recognize the distinctive voice of the we-narrator (probably Luke himself) in the description of the voyage (27:1—28:16), and he is an ideal travelling companion, with an innate sense of adventure awakened by the mechanics of the voyage itself, and a positive relish for the nautical details of ships and ports, winds and waves.

Coastal waters

The first stage means revisiting familiar waters along the southern coast of Asia Minor (modern Turkey: you'll need a map to get the full flavour of this voyage). Most shipping in the Roman empire was privately owned merchant shipping, taking on a few passengers to supplement the time-honoured business of transporting merchandise between the busy ports of the Mediterranean seaboard. So Julius' first task is to find a coastal trader to connect with the Roman shipping lanes further west (v. 2). Did the little ship from Adramyttium strike a homely note for the traveller who had first joined Paul at nearby Troas (16:10–11)? Then it's a matter of threading their way between island and shore, sailing in the lee of Cyprus to avoid contrary winds (v. 4), watching Cilicia and Pamphylia slip by, perhaps reflecting on all that had happened there—and finally disembarking at Myra (v. 5), where the boat from Adramyttium turns north up the Aegean coast and Julius has to find a ship to take the party west, across the open sea.

The Italian job

Greek seamanship drew on an age-old expertise in sailing coastal waters, but was much less confident in crossing the open sea towards Italy. There was, however, a regular trade supplying the voracious imperial city with its luxuries and its basics—top among which was grain. Enormous grain-ships from Egypt regularly made the hazardous crossing from Alexandria via the ports and islands of the southern Aegean. The emperor Caligula described them as 'crack sailing craft, their skippers the most experienced there are; they drive their vessels like race horses on an unswerving course that goes straight as a die' (Casson 1999, p. 158). This was the type of ship Julius found to transport his little group of prisoners to Italy (v. 6). Such a ship could take up to 1000 passengers (probably camping on deck), as well as a hold stuffed with grain (27:38), so there would be plenty of room for the 276 passengers that Luke mentions on this sailing (27:37). The real voyage is about to begin.

REFLECTION

'Some went down to the sea in ships, doing business on the
mighty waters; they saw the deeds of the Lord,
his wondrous works in the deep.'

Psalm 107:23–24

STORM & SHIPWRECK

A sea-voyage quickly takes on its own momentum. The ship becomes a microcosm, its own little world cut off from other kinds of reality—one in which the true dimensions of the physical and spiritual world assert their priority over the social and political structures that dominate life on land. Certainly, the authority of the physical world is very evident in Luke's description of this voyage into the unknown.

Running before the storm

First, we feel the contrary winds that keep the ship desperately beating against the wind (vv. 7–8), making heavy weather of a stage that should be a straight run to Crete. There is almost a sense of a physical force keeping Paul back from his divinely ordained destination, with the Fair Havens (one of the few natural harbours on the southern coast of Crete) a welcome shelter from the hostile forces of nature. Then comes the deceptive light wind (v. 13) that entices the ship's master to nose out from the relative safety of this shallow and exposed cove in a risky attempt to scuttle round to the north coast to find a safer shelter from the winter storms (v. 12)—only to be caught by the vicious blast of 'the typhoon known as Euraquilo' (v. 14) and swept out into the nameless horrors of the open sea, out of sight of land, without sun or stars to navigate by (v. 20).

Whose I am, and whom I serve

Life on board ship also shows up the true dimensions of spiritual authority. Paul has already shown himself a better judge of wind and weather than the professional sailors (vv. 9–10), although we can hardly blame Julius for trusting the professional expertise of the ship's master and his helmsman (v. 11). As the storm takes hold, there is a panic-stricken sense of the powerlessness of human skill and resource in the face of the relentless forces of nature (vv. 15–19). Gradually, Paul the prisoner emerges as the true leader of the beleaguered crew (vv. 21–32), but only by virtue of the fact that he too is a servant (v. 23).

Land ahead

Sailors often have a sixth sense that tells them there is land ahead, even in the dark (v. 27). That, however, brings a new danger. In the open sea, the preoccupation of the ship's crew is to keep the ship afloat and the right way up: hence the priority of getting rid of unnecessary gear (vv. 17–19). But with land—and a totally unknown land—ahead, the first priority is to prevent her running blindly aground (vv. 27–29). Taking soundings (v. 28) is done by the traditional method of swinging a line with a weight at the end to touch bottom. They are close enough, clearly, to run out four anchors from the stern (v. 29), and close enough for some of the sailors to think of making off to shore in the ship's dinghy, under the pretence of putting out anchors from the bows (v. 30). But the passengers will be helpless without the crew, and the ship's company must stay together (vv. 31–32). There is nothing to do but wait and see what day will bring (v. 33).

Jonah in reverse

There is a nice reversal here of the Jonah story. There, the whole ship's company is endangered by a prophet running away from his God (Jonah 1:7–16); here, the whole ship's company is saved by the presence of a prophet who is acting in obedience to his God (v. 24). In that context, there is a peculiar piquancy in the act of breaking bread and giving thanks to God on the swaying ship's deck, listening to the waves crashing on the reefs ahead (vv. 34–35). This is a powerful demonstration of moral authority coming from the most expendable person on board. The prisoner's calmness and refusal to panic have a beneficial effect on the whole crew (vv. 36–38). But Paul's action is also, in the deepest sense, sacramental, a celebration of eucharist—the thanksgiving of the whole created world to its Creator, enacted by the faithful remnant in the midst of and on behalf of the unbelieving micro-world with whom its fate is inextricably entwined.

REFLECTION

'Then they cried to the Lord in their trouble, and he brought them out from their distress; he made the storm be still, and the waves of the sea were hushed. Then they were glad because they had quiet, and he brought them to their desired haven. Let them thank the Lord for his steadfast love, for his wonderful works to humankind.'

Psalm 107:28–31

85   ACTS 27:39—28:6

DESERT ISLAND HOSPITALITY

Here, finally, is the emissary of the gospel, washed up on a desert island, bearing the signs of God's active presence with him—and finding unexpected hospitality from the island's inhabitants.

All safe to land

The ship's final traumatic moments are described in fascinated detail. The sailors abandon all attempts to control the ship by anchors or rudder, and trust that the onshore wind will bring her safely ashore on the sandy beach glimpsed beyond the breakers (v. 40). But the shallow bay has a deceptive 'double sea', a place of contrary currents caused by the underlying configuration of the seabed, and the ship finds herself trapped, bows rammed aground and stern being broken up by the force of the waves (v. 41). It's a moment of epic drama that calls forth echoes of the sea stories of Homer's *Odyssey*, known to every Greek schoolboy—but, for the prisoners, the chief danger comes from the soldiers (v. 42). Julius the centurion has to exert his authority to prevent Paul being summarily executed (v. 43), so there is a real sense of having escaped 'by the skin of our teeth' in the final words of this dramatic chapter (v. 44).

An island called Malta

But where are they? In Luke's story, this is an island in the farthest west, reached after storm and tribulation—an island peopled by 'barbarians' (v. 2), the patronizing Greek word for anyone who did not speak Greek. But Malta is home to one of the oldest civilizations in the world, and had been settled over the centuries by a variety of incomers. The native language was in fact a form of Punic, a relic of the centuries-old Phoenician colonization of the western Mediterranean. So the shipwrecked party find themselves surrounded by native islanders speaking an unintelligible language—a potentially hostile crowd, but still part of God's world and capable of mediating God's grace to the shipwrecked passengers and crew. Kindling a fire is the obvious priority for the soaked, shivering survivors (v. 2). It's raining (the only place in Acts where the weather is mentioned), and it's cold—not only because it is still early dawn (27:39), but because it was already autumn when the ship left Crete (27:9)—only two weeks ago—which means that winter is getting closer.

Bonfire night

In the flickering half-light, with unaccustomed bodies barging about in the undergrowth, it's no wonder the startled adder fastens on to Paul's hand as he gathers brushwood (v. 3), under the terrified gaze of the locals, who expect Paul to swell up or drop dead (v. 6). Like the pagan sailors on Jonah's ship (Jonah 1:7–10), they are only too ready to make connections between natural disaster and divine displeasure. It looks to them like a surefire proof that this particular prisoner was not meant to survive the shipwreck (v. 4). But their expectations couldn't be more wrong: Paul shakes the adder off, completely unharmed. There's now an instant switch from execration to hero-worship. In the public imagination, you're either a criminal or a god.

In the midst of the disaster, there is a wry humour about this episode, but Luke is making a serious point too. Paul is on trial for his life, his whole mission under scrutiny. We know from Paul's own letters that many of his fellow Christians were questioning his motives and doubting his divine calling when he was in prison (see Philippians 1:12–20). Many people today are equally ready to jump to conclusions when a star or public figure is overtaken by accident or illness, lurching from adulation to vilification. So Luke's story subtly conveys a deeper and more powerful verdict on Paul's mission than Caesar could ever do. God's servant is neither a criminal nor a god: he's a vulnerable human being, subject to the same winds and waves as the rest of us, but someone who has placed his life in the hands of the one who is utterly trustworthy (27:23).

REFLECTION

'By awesome deeds you answer us with deliverance, O God of our salvation; you are the hope of all the ends of the earth and of the farthest seas… You silence the roaring of the seas, the roaring of their waves, the tumult of the peoples. Those who live at earth's farthest bounds are awed by your signs; you make the gateways of the morning and the evening shout for joy.'

Psalm 65:5, 7–8

86

AND SO *to* ROME

Islands play a peculiar role in the Greek imagination, evoking both fear of the unknown and idyllic visions of a natural paradise. There is an element of that mixture in Paul's winter on Malta—a time out of time, making space for rest and restoration, a momentary glimpse of creation reunified and made whole.

Paul the healer

Malta is not a desert island: it has a 'first man' (local governor) with the very Roman name of Publius (v. 7). He has a country estate near to where Paul and his party are washed up, and offers hospitality for three days. Luke doesn't explain how this came about. 'Us' probably means not the whole crew but Paul the Roman citizen and his friends and fellow prisoners, an introduction probably effected under the watchful eye of Julius the centurion, who wastes no time in getting himself and his charges safe under a civilized Roman roof. Here at the ends of the earth, Paul finds hospitality—and Luke highlights the parallels with other hosts, and other healings, right back to the beginning of the Gospel story. Jesus' mission began with the prophetic proclamation of God's creation order restored (Luke 4:16–21), and his healing ministry in Capernaum began with the healing of his host's mother-in-law (Luke 4:38–39). Even as a shipwrecked prisoner, Paul is still an agent of that healing power (vv. 8–9). Here is further confirmation (if we needed it) that Paul's God is still with him, and a reminder that the healing that Jesus proclaimed was never confined to Israel (see Luke 4:24–27).

Romeward bound

This idyllic island life isn't where Paul's story ends, however. God has work for him to do in Rome. Rather incongruously, just over the island are the busy shipping lanes leading across to the ports of Sicily (vv. 12–13) and on to Italy. Generously supplied for the voyage by their new island friends (v. 10), all they have to do is to wait for the sailing season to open again in March and take the first ship heading across the straits to Rome (v. 11). This is another Alexandrian vessel, over-wintering on the island and sailing under the figurehead of the

Dioscuri or 'Heavenly Twins' ('Gemini' to modern astrologers). They were the patron deities of sailors and frequently appear in shipwreck stories, but Paul has no need of their protection. Our nautical diarist is enjoying the sense of being on the move again and relishing the details of ports and winds (vv. 12–13), but also, perhaps, marking with some nervousness every stage of the prisoner's journey to Rome to face again the problems he had been able to forget at sea. From Rhegium, the ship sails up the west coast of Italy to Puteoli, one of the major disembarkation points for the city (v. 13), and meets an unexpected grace: there are 'brothers' in Puteoli, Christian friends who offer hospitality and encouragement as the party pauses for another week (v. 14).

Journey's end

There is a real sense of achievement about the end of Paul's epic voyage: 'And that's how we got to Rome!' (v. 14). We have tracked across the Mediterranean, battling our way against contrary winds, battered by everything the sea can throw at us, and survived storm and shipwreck. So have we reached the 'ends of the earth' (1:8)? In a way, yes. Certainly Rome seems a long way away from Jerusalem (2:10), and the long sea-voyage of chapter 27 reinforces that impression. But there is also a surprising sense of homecoming about these last stages of the voyage, coming up the Appian Way past the Forum of Appius and the Three Taverns (v. 15), the final staging-posts on the road maps of the empire in which all roads lead to Rome. Word has got back from Puteoli about Paul's arrival, and there is a welcoming party coming to greet and escort the prisoner to Rome with all the ceremony of a visiting dignitary. We have got to the ends of the earth—but God is there before us.

PRAYER

'If I take the wings of the morning, and dwell in the uttermost parts of the sea, even there your hand will lead me, and your right hand shall hold me fast.'

Psalm 139:9–10

87

In MY END IS MY BEGINNING

The emissary of the gospel has finally reached Rome, but this final scene is not quite what we might expect. Rome already has a flourishing Christian community (28:15), and Paul arrives not as a missionary but as a prisoner, with the ever-watchful presence of a soldier to keep him in mind of the restrictions on his freedom (v. 16).

Meeting the Jewish community

The final scene of Acts shows Paul defending his position for the last time, not (as we might expect) before the emperor, but before the leaders of the local Jewish community (v. 17). They are the ones he is most concerned to meet and explain his position to—insisting that nothing he has done was intended to harm the interests of his own nation (vv. 18–19). Paul's underlying motivation, he insists (as he has done all through the trial chapters in Acts), is not treachery but loyalty—loyalty to Israel's deepest hopes and aspirations (v. 20). Equally interesting is the response of the community leaders (vv. 21–22): a measured neutrality regarding the actions of the Jerusalem authorities, and a genuine open-mindedness towards Paul's theological claims. Tell us about this sect, they say, for we have had no ruling about you from Jerusalem (v. 21); all we have is contradictory rumours about a sect that seems to attract bad publicity wherever it goes (v. 22). In a sense, that is the question to which Luke's whole narrative seeks to provide an answer: 'Tell us your story, tell us what this Jesus business is all about.'

Famous last words

The final scene of Acts (vv. 17–28) leaves us effectively where Luke's story of Jesus began, with the messenger of God's kingdom pleading, arguing, debating, testifying to his fellow Jews, seeking by every means possible to persuade his listeners about Jesus (v. 23)—but finding, just as John the Baptist did, that some are persuaded while others are not (v. 24; compare Luke 3:7–20). This is the tragedy that Luke's story ultimately faces: not a total rejection of the gospel, but a failure on the part of the community as a whole to grasp the opportunity on offer.

Like the Baptist and Jesus himself (Luke 3:4–6; 4:16–25), Paul finds himself falling back on the words of the prophet Isaiah to identify what is happening here, picking up those chilling words from Isaiah 6:9–10 that seem to suggest that some of God's people are simply incapable of hearing the word of God's salvation (vv. 26–27). This is another example of the early church's habit of using the 'that' of scripture to throw light on the 'this' of what is actually happening, to find scriptural precedent for the unfolding pattern of events (compare Luke 8:9–10). Although most of the first Christians were Jews, it is a fact that the churches failed to convince Israel as a whole to adopt their messianic view of history. We can see Paul wrestling with the same problem in Romans 9—11. This is not a judgment on Israel, much less a final 'turning away' from preaching to the Jews. It is Paul's justification for extending the preaching of God's kingdom to the Gentiles (v. 28), saying in effect, 'I've given you your chance; now you can't complain if I give them theirs too.' The bringing in of the Gentiles doesn't mean that God has rejected his people. By no means! (Romans 11:1).

Light to the Gentiles

That is the note on which Luke chooses to end his story. Acts doesn't come to a grand climax or a triumphalistic conclusion. Paul is still a prisoner, still awaiting a trial that may end in his death. The journey that began on the mountain-top, with the heavens opened and angels pointing the way, ends in a hired lodging in a back street in Rome (v. 30), where even the words of God's messenger are open to doubt and debate. It's the end of the story—but not the end of the journey. 'The story of God's purpose has not drawn to a close, but, quite the contrary, is manifestly still being written in the life of Jesus—then in Acts, in the life of the early Christian communities, and is now ongoing' (Green 1995, p. 28). The word is loose: it's out on the street—and nothing can stop it (v. 31).

REFLECTION

'Lord, now lettest thou thy servant depart in peace, according to thy word: for mine eyes have seen thy salvation, which thou hast prepared before the face of all people; a light to lighten the Gentiles, and the glory of thy people Israel.'

Luke 2:29–32